women.weaving.webs

Will Women Rule the Internet?

Dr. Clarisse Behar Molad

Dr. Clarisse Behar Molad

CBM Press
8106 Meadow Crest
Houston, TX 77071

Cover Design by Julie Parker
Cover Production by Mary Valle-Cooper
Interior Layout & Desigin by Rita Mills

ISBN# 0-9675835-0-0

women.weaving.webs

Table of Contents

My utmost gratitude to my friend Julie Parker,
without whom I would have never been able to write this book.

Also to Judy King my editor and
Rita Mills my publishing consultant,
many thanks for your kind advice.

And heart-felt thanks to my kids,
Leital, Danny, Shelley and Mickey, and
my parents for their
unlimited love and support.

Preface

A Hero in Our Midst

I met Hero online. She was featured in a story on CNN Online in September 1999. As I read the story, I realized that Hero stands for everything I believe is so amazing about the Internet and the reason I wrote this book. I contacted her that same day and asked her to re-tell me her story so I can share it with you. So here it is....

"I've got an unknown neuro developmental problem which has been described as 'locked-in syndrome'. I am not paralyzed but full of chaotic movement: profound apraxia of all muscles prevents independent voluntary control. I can't talk, walk, gesture, etc. It upsets me a great deal but it has to be lived with." says Hero. "I have small voluntary movements which are submerged under the huge involuntary chaotic tremors, lunges, tics and reflexes; small movements which can be felt by people who work hands-on with me, as my therapists have done since I was 15 months old. Hence, everything I do is enabled by trained carers, even communication and defecation. Most of the time my mother is my enabler."

"Writing is everything for me," says Hero, who spends most of her day in a wheelchair and has not attended school since she was 6. "Without writing I am nothing because everything I feel, think and need must be conveyed through my spelling." It is that love of writing—and meeting new people—that has made the Internet such a critical part of her life, she says.

"I got Internet facilities when I was clinically depressed after losing my place at the Royal Academy of Music where I had been for a year studying alongside undergraduates even though I was only 9. The Internet was fun, fun, fun. I found e-pals with disabilities and suddenly I had people who understood what I was up against. I invented my webzine *From The Window* and collected experiential articles and some poetry from my friends and acquaintances to get it started. I'm now on issue 6 and have had some success in persuading eminent persons such as John Tavener (now my godfather), George Carey, Melvyn Bragg, Margaret Atwood and Kofi Annan to write for it," Hero writes.

"It's got a readership in 89 countries and came first (£1,500!) in the individual category of the Cable & Wireless/ Childnet International 1999 Awards. They offered me a 4-day trip to Sydney to collect the prize but I raised £12,000 or thereabouts in sponsorship so I (plus dear old mum and a very good pal as carers) could trot to Africa, Asia and America as well as Australia for my first trip outside Europe. I journeyed into a new self with a new agenda, so slammed into hurtful reality was I by the poverty of real life individuals I met with in Tanzania and Bangladesh. I asked for a meeting with Kofi Annan and got it. I discussed water supplies and sanitation and he's encouraging me to agitate for improvements, to make use of my energy and talents...." Hero writes.

From the Window is deliberately kept graphically simple. "I had no complex software, was irritated by hopping and jumping about, wanted content, not vacuous superficial glitz and can't stand the time it takes to reach some sites which use a lot of graphics. It's also best for the blind the way it is." explains Hero. "Some people are unable to see past disability, see the whole of me. They ... fail to see the whole person is just the same as them." Her magazine is a way to show them what they risk overlooking.

When I asked Hero what the Internet meant to her, she wrote: "The internet is so much fun and so useful. It's one of the greatest inventions ever, like electricity, or the car. How can one do without it? It's only just beginning...." She added, "Just imagine in my own case. I've had 2,000 letters from 89 countries from complete strangers. I've used it to organize a trip to four continents, including the fund-raising. I've prepared the ground so that that journey could be accomplished despite my disability. And I'm in e-mail contact with some of the most powerful and interesting people of the day as well as daily contact with my less well known pals."

When I asked her to tell me what the future of the Internet holds for her and for the rest of humanity, she replied: "I look forward to shopping on the net for things that will be delivered to my door such as our groceries. When that takes off in the UK, urban sprawl and congestion could lessen and the endless number of acres given over to parking outside ugly warehouse type developments all around the edge of our old beautiful cities could be reduced. I don't see why it shouldn't lead to more beauty and less commercialism. It is wondrous how it frees individuals to connect. It's a very positive social thing, rather than an isolating one. It's a tool. It's what we use it for that counts. Of course some folk abuse it, just as they do guns or knives or their own brute strength, but, hey, you can just turn your back on it on the web and connect elsewhere with like-minded people. The political repercussions haven't begun yet. Bill Gates for king? or global village, global governance, people power? likely some balance betwixt the two."

I then asked what she would tell other girls her age about using the Internet, especially those with disabilities, and she emphasized: "Get connected, you're missing out. Use it as a tool to further what you do in life. It's not a substitute for other things but a supplement, an enriching, empowering tool. Interact. It's a pretty boring way to pass the time otherwise."

Finally I asked her if she were "ruling the Internet," what would she have done to make it better? And she answered, "I'd get rid of all the porn and make everybody in the world nice and sufficiently comfortable in their material possessions, but, hey, how can one do that?"

She concluded by saying, "Margaret Mead said it—Never doubt that a small group of thoughtful committed citizens can change the world: indeed it's the only thing that ever has.—Right!"

She can be found online at: www.fromthewindow.com

Introduction

Will Women Rule the Internet?

A *Wall Street Journal* ad from February 1998:

> # The end of the world as we know it....
> # 70 million women will do to the Net what they did to television.

"Media hype," you say. But is it?

We are currently in the midst of a revolution in communication technology, perhaps on the same scale as the invention of the printing press, the camera, the radio, or even reaching back to the development of written language. With widespread use of e-mail and the World Wide Web, we are experiencing drastic changes in how we communicate with each other and how we experience ourselves in relation to others. Some of us have taken quickly and eagerly to this new way of the world—others have held back and are approaching this new frontier with some trepidation and outright fear.

In what ways is the media of Internet serving our needs, and what needs remain to be served? What are the reservations, and perhaps the fears, of those who have not embraced the Internet? What are the dreams of those who already feel at home? Statistics show us that the Net has been male-dominated since its beginning. This is perplexing since the concept of the Internet can be particularly suited to a woman's way of acting—using cooperation, collaboration, sharing, and constant communication.

Women and Webs of Relationships

In 1997 I created the Women.Weaving.Webs project to give women a strong voice on the subject of the Internet. "How do we see it now, and how would we like to see it in the future?" are the kind of questions I asked women. And were they afraid to give me an answer! So through a series of seminars we provided women with a receptive and warm environment lacking any form of intimidation in order to encourage them to speak their mind and ask any questions they wished to ask about the Internet. They did ask a lot of questions, and they were eager to learn more and more!

It is the Women.Weaving.Webs project's premise that, unlike any other technology to date, the Internet—and its multimedia manifestation through the Web—is most suited to women's psychological profiles and makeup, yet paradoxically many women are still hesitant to use it. Furthermore, as the Web explodes globally beyond anyone's ability to measure its speed of deployment, women around the world are being left behind. Therefore, the project strived to enlighten the participants about the incredible match between women's interactions and the correlating structure of the Web. Its purpose was to accomplish a quantum leap in women's embrace of the Web and the opening of a new path to their success in working with Internet technology.

The wonderful fit between the female's makeup and the infrastructure of the Web can best be illustrated through the workings of Sally Helgesen, the noted author of *The Female Advantage*, who writes:

> The structure of the web of inclusion first presented itself to me when I tried to draw rough approximations of the organizations run by women .... What I came up with always bore a literal, architectural resemblance to a spider's web.... this interweaving made the structures inextricably integrated and connected—[it was a] pattern, really of relationships....
> Also like a spider's web, the structures were continually being built up, stretched, altered, modified, and transformed.... (from *The Web of Inclusion: Architecture for Building Great Organizations*)

Helgesen goes on to tell how she found out that, in the process of devising ways of leading that made sense to them, women had built profoundly integrated and organic organizations in which the focus was on nurturing good relationships; in which the niceties of hierarchical rank and distinction played little part; and in which lines of communication were numerous, open, and diffuse.

"I noted that the women tended to put themselves at the centers of their organizations rather than at the top," she writes, "thus emphasizing both accessibility and equality, and that they labored constantly to include people in their decision making."

There was no recognized name or category for what

the women were doing, so Sally Helgesen began referring to their organizations as "webs of inclusion."

When women realize how the World Wide Web mirrors the way they think and operate, they will begin to understand what a powerful hold we women can take of this new technology. I strongly believe that women can become the most sophisticated users and architects of the Internet! Since the Internet is still in its infancy, now is the time for women to get in at the ground level and help shape the future uses of this incredible form of communication.

The Internet is helping shape areas of society that women have excelled in for centuries, such as community building and trade and commerce. Women have always been the foundation upon which villages' lives were conducted. In the virtual village, women can once more become the prominent builders of the new society. Women can use their considerable ease of communicating and reach out to other women all over the world to form a unity of vision that can help us achieve what was impossible yesterday.

For the first time, since technology has started revolutionizing our lives, we have a technology that we can feel most comfortable with, just like we embraced the telephone. It is now hard to believe that when the telephone was first invented, it was envisioned strictly as a business tool and considered to have no use for the home where women spent their time. With Internet use slowly penetrating many countries and Internet communication being so rich yet so affordable, women can draw upon their strong abilities to share and collaborate and make a great impact in many areas of life. We can affect the way we handle the global environment, we can build new alliances to deal with children's and women's health, we can strengthen our educational resources, and—finally—we can become the new merchants and buyers of the virtual marketplace.

Chapter 1

How Can Women Shape, Lead, and Prosper from the Internet?

It is 1982 and I am sitting across the table from four guys at a Texas Instruments (TI) office in Lubbock, Texas. TI has asked me to provide them with a list of ideas for new software to run on their successful TI-99 home computer. After months of research I have come up with several software ideas, identified the appropriate content designers, and made contact with a couple of programmers to develop the first prototypes. And now I am here to show the TI executives the fruits of my labor.

At the head of the table sits the newly appointed head of the Home Computing Division. The division is small in comparison to other TI departments but is rumored to be growing rapidly. He is wearing his cowboy clothes and his booted legs are resting on the table in front of him. Today I am pitching an idea for a girls' magazine. My research has shown that girls are not keeping up with boys when it comes to using computers. Mind you, there are very few computers in the market—the Apple II, the Commodore 64, the Atari, and the TI 99. And the market it still very small. However, the gender split is already showing.

The TI-99 computer is very affordable and easy to use.

It is not yet associated with arcade gaming like the Atari machine, so there is a good chance it will be perceived as just as attractive to girls as it is to boys. The idea of the magazine is very simple: Develop interactive content that middle-school girls can relate to—about fashion, relationships, school, and the like. Our biggest problem is devising a plan to entice girls to buy new versions of the magazine on a regular basis. However, TI has a solution to that. They have a 99er's club that customers become a member of when they buy a TI computer. Members can swap software cartridges via mail with other members or with TI itself, who will recycle the used cartridges.

I am very confident that I have discovered a vast untapped market for TI and can't wait to see the reaction of the VP. After my presentation and short enthusiastic demo, he stretches his legs further on the table and growls with a heavy Texas accent, "What good is a magazine if you can't take it to the john?" Everybody is silent for a moment and then slowly the men all start laughing. As they continue laughing, I look at them with total disbelief and realize I have reached a dead end.

New Vision

TI is no longer in the home computing business. They decided to quit the business altogether a few months after they signed a substantial contract with me to develop a series of software programs, which did not include the teen girls' magazine. I found out about it on a Friday evening while listening to the 10:00 o'clock television news. I was not able to salvage my TI-proprietary software prototypes to covert them to run on other PC platforms. My dream of being a trailblazer for girls' software went up in smoke....

Today, almost 20 years later, I listen to people like Laura

Groppe from Girl Games, Inc. and know that this story has not yet reached a happy ending. Laura has been working very hard in the last five years to develop computer games for girls. She also has a magazine that members of her girls' club get free when they join the club. Updates are available on the Internet. Her ideas are very much in keeping with my former ones, but even with the new technologies and bigger audience, she has not made it to the big leagues. All the major hard copy magazines also have Web versions of their magazines today. They all have acknowledged that teen girls represent a lucrative market and realize that these girls can easily be reached online, but their actual number is still smaller than the number of boys who use the Internet.

I found my marketing and design notes about the girl e-zine 18 years later after starting my second computer consulting business. I read the notes with amazement as to how far I was willing to go to pursue my dream to get more girls and women to learn to love computers. I suddenly recalled meeting with a representative from *Ladies Home Journal* in 1982 to discuss the possibility of distributing samples of my software programs via a floppy disk attached to the magazine. I was adamant I would find a way to spread the word to women magazine readers that a new dawn is emerging and that they ought to become part of the new computing revolution. I wanted them all to experience this through simple programs about interesting topics like travel, so they would all rush and buy computers.

It took me 15 more years of working in the information technology field before I felt the same enthusiasm again. It happened when a friend gave me a beta copy of the Mosaic browser and exclaimed, "You will not believe this!" All of a sudden, my PC was transformed to an amazing communication vehicle and I was flying high in cyberspace. Within minutes of venturing into the World Wide Web, I felt right at home. And once I did, I wanted to share it with everybody I knew. But most of all, I wanted to share it with all those women I had tried to reach in 1982, who have been resisting the lure of the computer.

I went on to meet many wonderful women in computing during my travels around the world. I was moved when I listened to their stories and told them I will share them with their systers in the U.S. Here are some of them:

Nadia

Her name is Nadia. She is 24 years old. I met her in late 1998 while she assisted me in presenting a lecture about the Internet to a room full of eager people in Kotor, somewhere in Eastern Europe. She knows nothing about barriers to women in technology. After all, she has a bachelor's degree in computer science and is a Web master at a large oil and gas company. Nadia could be the one living and working in Houston, Texas. Instead, she lives in a small country called Montenegro on the beautiful coast of the Adriatic Sea. She loves the Web and has been excited about developing YUGO Petrol's Web site from the minute someone showed her how to write HTML code. She has built the Web site using all the bells and whistles she has seen on other sites from the Western world, yet she knows that her accomplishment may be short-lived. After all, she has the job for only six months and, by the end of the year, might find herself back on her parents' farm, taking care of their pigs.

Nadia giggles when I tell her about the book. She, of course, would love to be part of the "ruling class" of the Internet. However, she says she has never experienced discrimination as a woman in computing. Nadia was an average student at her Montenegro State University. In Montenegro there is no visible gender difference when it comes to the sciences. She could have studied anything she wanted. Whether she could find a job after graduating was another story. Luckily she landed a short-term assignment.

Her country's borders are closed for people like Nadia due to the ongoing international embargo. She lives off $200 a month, most of it going to Mom and Dad on the farm. But she always has the Internet. In cyberspace she can go anywhere anytime. Nadia goes to her job at the oil and gas company with great anticipation everyday. How far will she travel virtually today? She dreams of a day when she will be able to own a computer with an Internet access. I suggest to Nadia, "Maybe you should start doing contract Web design for other companies in Montenegro?" and she giggles again. The notion of having that much control over her future is bizarre for her. Right now, her only hope for the future is that there will be no war. Then she might have the chance to stay at YUGO Petrol and continue to work on the Web site she so beautifully constructed.

Women like Nadia are not hard to find. In Eastern Europe, where the sciences are a common area for women to master, computers (perceived mostly as a scientific tool) are as available to women as they are to men. Business is different, though. In the business world, women use computers mostly as enhanced typewriters. The Internet introduces a whole other realm to those women. It represents the connection to the West. Just like MTV, the local McDonald's, and Levi's jeans, the Internet in Eastern Europe is fashionable for young women. Maybe because so many of these young women have a solid understanding of the sciences, they are willing to look beyond the end user's perspective and venture into the guts of this super network and the systems supporting it. In countries such as Bulgaria, Macedonia, Yugoslavia, Slovenia, Croatia, and Romania, one sees young women working side by side with young men, in small Internet companies, writing code and managing networks.

Nevertheless, when surveying the demographics of Net users across Eastern Europe, the typical profile invariably remains that of a young male, fresh out of college, with an engineering degree. Young males are the ones aggressively seeking Internet access in any position they hold, whether with a small or large company. They are the ones willing to go the distance in exploring even illegal means to connect to the Internet at as low a cost as possible. They are not the geeks—they are the hip few with a constant open window to the Western world.

Sanja

Another example of women embracing the Internet is Sanja, from Macedonia. I met her in late 1996 when she assisted with another one of my Eastern European lectures about the Net. Sanja was 25. Despite her lack of high-tech knowledge, she had just been hired to work at the first private ISP (Internet service provider) of her country—most likely because she was the girlfriend of one of the programmer/hackers (in Macedonia, the term "hacker" is worn as a badge of honor). Sanja was best at surfing the Net. She spent endless hours doing so and knew much more about what's "out there" than many of her American counterparts who do not have time to do so. She lived at home with her parents, but her life was with the company. She spent all her time there, either working or taking advantage of being part of the emerging Macedonian culture of the lucky few who could afford to hook up to the

Net at any time.

Sanja told me she loved her work. She was a civil engineer by profession, but there were no jobs to be found in her field so she hung around the ISP as a jack-of-all-trades in the hope that she could stay there for awhile. She did not share the deep commitment that her male coworkers had to the company. She did not see herself becoming a future shareholder of the company. She had no special aspirations and did not spend too much time thinking about the possible role she might be playing as a technology pioneer in her country as well as in her region of the world.

Vera

Vera was the librarian at the American Embassy in Sofia, Bulgaria. It was 1997, and she had just connected the three PCs in her library to the Internet. Full of enthusiasm, she talked to me about all the great research opportunities she could now offer to anyone coming to the library. Vera herself had learned about the Internet by trial and error. She was very proud to be one of the few in the city to have unlimited access to what it has to offer. Her English was rather good, so she could surf and learn much faster than many of her colleagues.

Vera knew the Internet gave a whole new dimension to her job as a librarian. She hung out with the Americans from the embassy and read the American trade journals they brought to the library. On the day we were supposed to have a seminar in the library, the phone lines went dead. She looked at me with embarrassment and shrugged, "This is Bulgaria. Nothing is ever dependable." Then she told the workshop invitees they could go home and offered me a cup of coffee....

Maria

It was 1998 and I was in Japan giving another series of lectures. My interpreter was a woman I had met on my last trip there, so we felt like we were old friends. Maria was born in Japan but grew up in Canada. She came back to live in Japan as a young adult. She lives a traditional Japanese life as a wife, mother, and daughter-in-law (in a typical Japanese household, a mother-in-law lives with her family). After a long day of lecturing, we both sat quietly to have a cup of coffee at my hotel lobby.

"You know," said Maria, "I have a small business on the Internet." I could not have been more surprised! After all, women in Japan—especially middle-aged women—rarely have access to computers. As for the Internet, women are a tiny minority when it comes to the Japanese Net demographics.

"What do you do on the Internet?" I asked.

"Well," she said, "I got a license to distribute California wines in Japan and I have put up a Web site to try and sell them that way."

She smiled bashfully and went on to say, "My husband hates it when I get on the Internet at night. And my mother-in-law has threatened not to cook for my kids if I continue to put work before my family." Maria still considers herself an interpreter and not a Net entrepreneur. Japan at that time had the lowest number of women on the Internet of any industrialized nation, yet at the Tokyo Cyber Café I visited, young women dominated the scene. They laughed together as they sent e-mails to their friends and looked at the few sites available in Japanese.

One young woman working there explained the situation to me, "This is the only place we can come to have access to the Internet. In schools and at most of the homes, it is only the men who get to play with the computers. Computers and the Net access are still expensive, so it is the men who get to use them first."

Aliza

Across the ocean a year later, in late 1997, I organized a symposium at a Houston community center on the topic of women and the Internet. Aliza Sherman, the famous Cybergrrl (one of the first women site owners on the web), came in, followed by a vice president from Girl Games, Inc. We had exactly 14 people in the audience. None of them had heard of Cybergrrl or Girl Games. We discussed the need for women to get actively involved in using the Internet and all the benefits that involvement can bring to their lives. Our audience was not very enthusiastic.

About six months later Aliza's book that was a web guide for women came out and she was interviewed everywhere on television and the radio. A couple of women who came to the symposium stopped me at the community center and asked, "Hey, isn't she the one who was just here? You know, I really have to get on the Internet. My husband is online all the time, but I, of course, can never find the time to sit down and learn how to use it."

Today Aliza is considered our spokesperson on the web. She was a leader then and still remains one.

Women Are Getting the Message

The same year we held the symposium, we also ran a

workshop for 75 middle-school girls. I talked to them at length about the reason they should look at the Internet as a challenge they should all master. Some of them had used e-mail and told me proudly that they considered themselves "real experts," but when I asked them who got to go online more—they or their brothers/guy friends—they all yelled, "They do! They always want to play their stupid games!" My own daughter, Shelley, sitting in the midst of the group, looked away. She knew the same was true in our own house.

A year later Shelley demanded access to her own computer so she could get on the Internet. She still mostly uses e-mail but has ventured frequently onto the Internet to do research for her schoolwork. She still does not understand her younger brother's talk about "downloading" and "plug-ins," but she is no longer ignorant. She claims she wants to be a screenwriter when she grows up, yet she does not seriously contemplate the role the Internet might play in her future career.

In late 1998 I visited one of the most successful organizations Cybergrrl and Aliza Sherman have given birth to—the Webgrrls group in San Francisco. I spent the evening visiting with the founders of the group and many of the women who came to attend the evening's seminar. Valerie, the group's spokesperson, told me that a lot of the Webgrrls are former media/advertising professionals who are now freelancers doing Web design. These Web-savvy young women (all in their 20s or early 30s) form a hip group that effortlessly attracts new members (membership is free). When asked whether they consider themselves to be true Internet experts, Valerie hesitates in her answer, "Of course many of us do not have technical backgrounds. Very few of us have college degrees in technically related fields. We came to the Web because of our design backgrounds and, frankly, because we live in a city that knows more about the Net than any other city in the world."

There were about 100 women at the meeting. I asked one of them about her technical background. She is a contractor, with a solid background in network technologies. "Most companies are hesitant to hire a woman contractor for a purely technical assignment, but those that do are always telling me how much they loved working with me because I am not as arrogant as the guys...."

When I asked several of the women if they were planning on using their unique place as pioneers in Internet technology to start their own companies, all of them said no. They want to have the freedom of working for themselves, but not the burden of running a company.

I started the Women.Weaving.Webs project because I wanted to inspire more women to become power players in the Internet world. I did not care if they ended up as superusers or actual architects of the technology. I just wanted to share with my systers everywhere my sense of awe of the revolution I was experiencing firsthand. If there is one thing I have learned in my diverse career, it is that knowledge is power. The Internet is a technological revolution that is changing the way we work and live. The more we as women know about it, the better prepared we will be for the future and the stronger our stand will be in defining that future.

I invited anyone who cared to listen to me to come to the workshops I organized in various locations around Houston during 1996-1997. I tried not to teach technical skills at the workshops, but rather to motivate and encourage. I did not always succeed. Many times I was asked, "Why can't you just teach us how to do a search on the Internet?" But sometimes I hit a home run when women came to me months later and announced, "Guess what? I now have my business on the Net" or "Our organization is now all on e-mail. We communicate constantly rather than during our monthly meetings."

There are times I give lectures to a room full of women eager to learn everything about Net commerce. And there are other times I still face a half-empty room trying to deliver a message to companies that women are the best online marketing target they can have. I was recently invited to go to China and speak to women about the Net. The invitation, though, came with a little hint: "As you know, computer science and industry are developing rapidly in China. More and more people are involved in electronic commerce and the Internet; however, there are still many women *and men as well* who have never touched a computer. Your seminars will surely be warmly welcomed by women and China Women's Association for Science and Technology members," the letter of invitation said.

As I continue my travels, whether virtual or real, I always keep in mind that we, as women, have just begun our journey into the world of the Internet, yet I know for a fact that as the pace of change accelerates within that world, we must not pause after any accomplishment. We must push forward hard and use every gain to our advantage.

Chapter 2

Women's Numbers on the Net Are Soaring

The Women.Weaving.Webs conducted an online survey in late 1998. Ther Net, that was once a novelty, has become a necessity for many women who answered our survey. The goal of the survey was to get a sense of what women are thinking about the issues we have raised during our workshops. Most of the women who responded to the survey, however, were well acquainted with the World Wide Web. We were not able to reach out to the novices, and the results of the survey reflect that. Yet the results do give us a glimpse into the thoughts of female Web users regarding the role the Web is playing and will play in women's lives.

The majority of the respondents use the Internet more than five hours per week. Those who use it less than one hour per week said that was because of time constraints. All those who feel they need to learn more about the Internet said they were willing to do so. Most said they would self-teach or rely on peers to help them learn. When asked if they would like to use the Internet more than they presently do most said yes, but a significant number responded no. A typical comment was, "It's not difficult to learn how to use the Internet. It takes only curiosity and of course an Internet connection and PC. I was much more excited about the Internet 12 months ago as I was learning all the wonderful things I could access using it. Now it's basically a research tool, both at the office and at home."

Why Women Use the Net

When it comes to actual uses of the Internet, those surveyed said they spend most of their online time using e-mail. One respondent explained why, "One of my main uses is e-mailing friends and relatives. I find e-mail to be far more effective and personal than phone or letter. I've rekindled friendships in the past couple of years that had deteriorated into a letter at Christmas that have now resulted in personal visits and closer ties."

The next most frequent use was "visiting favorite Web sites." "Finding specific information for immediate practical use" was the highest rated favorite Internet activity with "communicating with friends and family" as a close second. Other activities such as entertainment, news, and online shopping received very few votes.

Communication and research were cited as the Internet's best function rather than entertainment or commerce. One of the comments that was made was "Internet shopping/commerce does not include the social/recreation components of shopping, so will never match 'real shopping.'" The participants rated "learning about new things" as what they would most like to use the Internet for in the near future, followed by "promoting my business" and "community involvement."

Recognizing the Gender Gap

A large majority thought that the percentage of women

Internet users and online shoppers would change in the next few years and felt it is "very important" that women have equal or better knowledge of technology compared to men. A comment reflecting this notion was "I would like to see girls in grade school encouraged more—they still are not taking math and science and computer usage in any great number. Parents, especially fathers, need to encourage their daughters to access the Internet, and computer 'games' need to be designed with young women in mind."

Another comment shows the real promise the Internet offers: "My daughter is on the Internet every night. I can see the difference in her knowledge and interest in computers and my own experiences. She has learned so much at an earlier age that I did. She has no fear of being on a computer and communicating with others on the Internet or searching for information she is interested in."

The majority responded they strongly agree that the Internet presents an opportunity for the gender gap to close. "The Net helps close the gender gap because of its anonymous, faceless nature. People are not judged by appearance, height, weight, gender, physical handicap, etc.... but more on how they use the technology and are able to communicate," stated one of the women.

Internet's Weaknesses

Most of the respondents described the Internet as something they are benefiting from presently and will benefit from in the future. The number one dislike of the Internet was pornography and the second was the fact that the Internet seems "disorganized, not easy to navigate." A high response was given also to "lack of privacy" and "too many advertisements." One comment summarized well the concerns about pornography: "The Internet has far outpaced our legislatures and government bodies as a whole, leaving gaps in accountability for what could not be legally published or permitted elsewhere. Example: There is legislation concerning pornography and 'hate' information distribution and access for printed materials, yet all a child has to do is to lie on a brief questionnaire (if one is even required) and he has access to anything and everything. I feel that to keep the idea of the Web alive and viable to the general public at large, this problem will have to be addressed."

Internet's Strengths

The respondents rated (in this order) the Internet as an effective means for

1. Education
2. Commercial use
3. Promoting and sharing ideas
4. Bringing down international barriers,
5. Community building

One comment goes so far as to say, "The Internet is the most important instrument of social change since the Industrial Revolution. The ability to work effectively away from an office environment will allow all kinds of changes in society, from where people live to how their work is done." The majority responded that they would like to see the Internet used for "providing education to remote locations" in the near future. One of the respondents also said, "The Internet is a wonderful tool to foster collaboration among women!"

When asked about use of the Net for creating their own

Web presence, the majority responded that they thought it was "very easy" or "somewhat easy" to create a Web site. The majority also agreed that the success that women have received through being published, discovered, promoting themselves, etc. on the Internet was one of its most important functions. When asked if any barriers they currently experience to creating their own Web presence can be overcome, 91 percent responded yes. In addition, one of the respondents felt that "perhaps a program where girls could build their own Web sites would be a start" to helping close the gender gap in computing. Furthermore, one woman noted, "These days I tend to think of a company as lightweight, lacking, possibly bogus, behind the times, etc.… if they do not have a Web site. Whether or not I actually place the order from the Net, I want to know that a company has a Web site, that I can research their product on the Net, and that I can communicate with them by e-mail."

Finally the majority claimed that they were "very excited" by the possibilities the Internet has to offer. The following comment sums it up: "I have used the Internet for many personal and professional things. Believe it or not, I found my wonderful husband and planned most of our wedding over the Internet. I shop personally and shop for work over the Internet. I plan trips, purchase tickets, look for real estate, watch stock—in a nutshell, it has changed my life!"

Recent Progress of Women on the Net

Today the number of women on the Web worldwide continues to climb. Compare the following statistics on reports over just the last few years:

In March 1995 *Computer-Mediated Communication Magazine,* in its article "Women on the Web" stated, "Demographically speaking, women constitute a minority in cyberspace; estimates of the Internet's female users begin at 15 percent of the total online population. Print publications have seized this phenomenon and painted a picture of the Internet and the Web as hostile territory; for instance, the youth-oriented women's magazine - featured an article stipulating that a woman can find happiness on the Net only by masking her gender."

Three years later, in January 1998, a South African online survey revealed that the amount of women online in South Africa alone represented 19 percent, up 3 percent from the previous year. The average amount of women online was 22 percent in Europe and 38 percent in the U.S. In Australia, of the 3 million Internet users that year, 1.7 million were male and 1.3 million were female.

By the middle of 1998, Georgia Tech University, who has been conducting surveys on the Internet for more than nine years, declared that, for the first time that year, females outnumber men in the new users category. Their poll showed that females accounted for 52 percent of all Internet users who been online for less than a year. While there were more women in this category than men, the overall statistic for women online remained at 38.7 percent, the same figure as last year's survey. The study also found that 43.8 percent of all users age 11 to 20 were women. The Internet remains predominantly white: 87.4 percent of users describe themselves as white, 3.1 percent Asian, 1.8 percent black, 1.5 percent Hispanic, 0.8 percent Latino, and 0.5 percent indigenous.

At the same time, NUA Surveys in its Pro Active Study, described the average Dutch Internet user (out of 1.5 million Dutch online) as 87 percent male, relatively young, aged 34, and typically both well educated and well salaried.

In the United States, however, Women Connection Online reported in July 1998 that the demographic profile of

Net users has become more like that of the U.S. population as a whole in age, gender, and marital status. "The Web isn't mainstream quite yet, but it's certainly moving in that direction," states Sam Alfstad, publisher of *eMarketer*, which did the report. Looking forward, the report revealed a continued mirroring effect with the Net population becoming even more similar to the overall public profile, an even greater percentage of women online and a massive movement to the Net among older Americans, both in sheer numbers and as a percentage.

The ratio of women to men online continued to be a topic of controversy among media and research groups reporting on Net user demographic trends in the following months. Women, as a percentage of total users online, grew from 33 percent in 1996 to 39 percent by year-end 1997, and they were projected to rise to 51 percent of users by the year 2002. Finally, in September of 1998, *Forbes* magazine published an article based on a Nielsen Media Research and Commeclude the social/recreation components of shopping, so will never match 'real shopping.'" The participants rated "learning about new things" as what they would most like to use the Internet for in the near future, followed by "promoting my business" and "community involvement."

Recognizing the Gender Gap

A large majority thought that the percentage of women Internet users and online shoppers would change in the next few years and felt it is "very important" that women have equal or better knowledge of tech that women, not men, may embody the most enticing online congregation yet.

Across the pond, a United Kingdom Survey by Ziff-Davis and Dell Computer in November 1998 confirmed that

40 percent of newcomers to the Net in the U.K. are female, helping to redress the male/female ratio. The fastest growing group of users was found to be among people aged 14-17 years, 47 percent of whom were female. At the same time in Finland–the "most wired country in the world"—a Gallup Media study announced that 41 percent of all Finns, some 1.79 million people, aged 12 and over, had gone online in 1998. But, as in most other countries, Finnish males outnumbered females in Internet usage. Of those who said they were frequent users, 60 percent were male.

By the end of 1998 the news got even better. America Online/Roper Starch released their Cyberstudy, which claimed, "Women have sparked the growth of Internet online in the last 12 months—accounting for 57 percent of the new home online subscribers during that period. This recent trend has boosted the women's share of the interactive medium to 47 percent."

When the new year emerged, a CNN report, "What to expect in PCs & the Web in 1999," declared, " Global Internet users will soar to 147 million—more than the population of Japan…. The Fourth Annual Predictions report by Frank Gens, a senior vice president for Internet research at IDC, also forecasts that "there will be more U.S. women than men using the Internet." Concurrently, A study released by Zona Research announced that "men outspent women this holiday season by an average of $707 to $543, but women's online buying went into overdrive, leaping 308 percent over last year compared with an increase by men of 145 percent."

By June of 1999 a CommercNet press release made it official:

WOMEN GAINING MOMENTUM—For the first time in two years, more online purchases are being made by women, reflecting a 9 percent growth since last summer. The number of women buyers increased more than 100 percent in four of the top five purchasing categories: those who purchased books increased 105 percent, CDs/videos 145 percent, clothing 118 percent, and computer hardware 160 percent. The fifth purchasing category, travel, had an increase of 63 percent....Nearly half of the Internet users are women. With online purchasing becoming easier, the majority of online shoppers are very likely to become online purchasers. Women have played a major role in that trend, and we expect to see them continue to lead the way.

Women are gaining ground in all areas of Internet usage as they overcome their fear and discover a medium that complements their way of thinking and relating to the world.

Chapter 3

The Commercial Lure of Women to Become Online Consumers

Women Shoppers Head to the Web in Force

As the Number of Internet Buyers Jumps 40% in Nine Months

New CommerceNet/Nielsen Media Research Study Also Shows Internet Users Top 92 Million in the U.S. and Canada

NEW YORK—June 17, 1999—The number of Internet users in North America has now reached 92 million, and the commercial growth of the Web is emerging as a dominant trend in the development of the Internet. According to an April 1999 study released today by CommerceNet and Nielsen Media Research, the number of Internet users age 16 and older in the U.S. and Canada increased 16 percent in just nine months, yet the number of online consumers jumped 40 percent to 28 million during the same period. The increase in the adoption of the Internet by consumers is, for the first time, being driven by women as the number of female consumers online jumped 80 percent in nine months and passed the 10-million mark.

Other Study Highlights:

Of today's 92 million Internet users, 46 percent are women. The percent of female users had been about 43 percent for nearly two years. Forty-one percent of today's 55 million Internet shoppers are women. This figure had been approximately 36 percent for nearly two years.

It is time to recognize that the notion of the Internet as a bastion of men is an outdated myth. More than half of the new users since 1996 have been women, according to a 1999 study by the Pew Research Center. More than half of America Online users are now women. Couple this trend with the greater buying power that women have as the primary manager of household budgets or as single heads of households, and women become a highly desirably audience on the Internet. Women do buy more than men on the Internet, as shown in research by Bruskin/Goldring. The highest percentage of women shoppers spends $100 to $200 per purchase whereas the highest percentage of male shoppers spends $25 to $50.

It is not just the stereotypical Internet-savvy young who are using the Internet, as evidenced by the fact that 45 percent of Web users are age 40-plus, according to *Business Week*. In fact, for women, the likelihood of Web use on a daily basis tends to increase with age. Women over 50 are the most likely to be accessing the Net daily, according to a study by CommerceNet/Nielsen.

Although online financial services have not traditionally been areas where women dominated usage, in the age group of 16 to 24 women were more than twice as likely as their male counterparts to have checked their bank balances online, according to CommerceNet/Nielsen. Think of the possible implications as this group grows older and gains in buying power!

Sixty-five percent of online shoppers are over 40, according to Ernst & Young, which may be explained by the tendency for both Web usage and buying power to increase with age. Internet gender statistics get even more interesting when buying power is factored in. The result is that older women online, with their purchasing clout and disposable income, represent a more attractive audience than younger users today.

Also women are starting businesses at twice the rate of men (Bureau of Labor Statistics 1997). By the year 2000 women will own 80 percent of new businesses, according to Women Consumer network, and they will control 40 to 50 percent of all companies in America, according to *Working Woman*.

Women like one-stop shopping with the ability both to access information and to act on it. Convenience is an imperative to today's busy professional women online, but it is considered valuable only when offered with all the information needed to make an informed buying decision.

Women's Portals

Women's portals (the Web megasites that serve as gateways to the Web and centralize a lot of content for a particular audience) are gaining quickly in popularity because portals are being recognized as tools that can help users master the information overload of the Internet and in women's lives. Portals also deliver a paradigm shift in transforming the information-gathering process from active to passive, thus saving time, improving productivity, and producing more valuable information content for better decision making. For example, rather than checking a particular stock every half-hour until it reaches a price at which you want to trade, you can have the system notify you automatically.

The most popular women's portal sites are:

- *iVillage.com* which offers a wide array of topics geared to women, from astrology, books, and fitness and health to parenting—and also some information about careers. With $6.5 million in revenues reported in the first quarter of 1999 and a staggering IPO (initial public offering) experience, iVillage is a beacon of women's portals. It also has equity investment from AOL and NBC. Its new NBC network partnership will result in prime time advertising that should be a boon to its traffic and subsequently to its advertising revenues.

- *women.com* which also covers a wide variety of topics. Women.com Networks was formed in early 1999 as a 50-50 joint venture between women.com and Hearst Corporation's HomeArts, which are the second and third most visited women's sites on the Web after iVillage. As a result, women.com's content looks like an online newsstand, fueled by its relationship with Hearst Publishing, which is responsible for such magazines as *Good House-keeping, Cosmopolitan,* and *Prevention.*

- *womenconnect.com* which is a newer site, targeting women in business. This site draws its content from MacDonald Communications Corporation's publications and features *Working Woman, Working Mother, National*

Journal's Hotline, and *InteliHealth*. In addition to featuring news on business and careers, the site also spotlights money, politics, travel, and health, with a strong thrust towards online shopping through its advertisers.

- *women.msn.com* which began in early 1999 and is Microsoft's answer to tapping into the women's online community. Using content from women.com, this site covers a multitude of topics.

- *Oxygen Media, Inc.* which was founded in 1998 by former Disney and Nickelodeon executive Geraldine Laybourne and has its capital from AOL and Disney/ABC. It is targeting women through both the Internet and cable television with original content focusing on health and family. Oxygen is a potent example of the potential players which are likely to emerge from the convergence of publishing, media, advertising, the Internet, and television. The company plans to launch its cable network in 2000 and already has three Internet sites: Thrive, Moms Online, and Electra.

With this proliferation of women's portals, it is clear that the business world is preparing the ground for women to become the drivers of Internet commerce. A press release on the new Oxygen Web site (www.oxygenmedia.com) states:

Oxygen Media announced today that it will launch a finance, business and careers Web site—and create related, integrated television programming—to address the most important financial issues for women. The new Web site—which will launch in mid-1999—and its related television programming adds to Oxygen's growing cluster of properties that comprise a comprehensive *home base* for women online and on television, and are the foundation of a new brand for women. The new finance, business and careers Web site will be integrated with Oxygen's existing and future online properties for women—Thrive, Moms Online, Electra and Oprah Online—and with the new Oxygen cable network that will launch on January 1, 2000. Geraldine Laybourne, Chairman and CEO of Oxygen said, 'This will be Oxygen's first *home-grown* Web site and the first comprehensive television programming devoted exclusively to women and money. That this is our first new initiative is a reflection of the growing and vital importance of women to the American economy, and the importance of finance and business to women.'

Companies Discovering Women's Market on Web

Has corporate America finally woken up to discover the women's market on the Web? Andy Wang from the *E-Commerce Times* wrote on July 20, 1999:

The competition is fierce among leading online women's networks with major players like iVillage (Nasdaq: IVIL), Oxygen and Women.com battling for eyeballs and dollars. iVillage just added a little more ammo.

Monday, e-commerce fashion site Styleclick.com (Nasdaq: IBUY) announced that it has signed a deal with iVillage to host a co-branded shopping area. Under the terms of the deal, Styleclick.com, which offers women's and men's fashions and personal shopping, will integrate its content directly into iVillage's existing shopping infrastructure.

'It has been reported that 70 million women will be online by the year 2000,' said Joyce Freedman, Styleclick.com's chairman and co-CEO. 'As such, women are the most valuable, sought-after demographic on the Internet. Women control the majority of household finances, are extremely brand-loyal, and make the majority of all purchasing decisions.'

Looking back, in August 1998 CommerceNet/Nielsen Media research indicated that the proportion of female Internet users had leveled off at 43 percent of Internet users—a slim increase from last year's 42 percent. Based on that survey, there were some 34 million female Internet users. However, while women have near parity in use, the survey said, they lag in online shopping. Among online shoppers, 71 percent of purchasers are men. All this is starting to change: in the 1998 holiday season, almost 750,000 women made their first online purchase, according to a report conducted by the Internet Research Group for AOL. The latest 1999 CommerceNet survey reveals:

WOMEN NOW DRIVING INTERNET BUYING—The new Internet Demographics study reveals that women are now the driving force in the growth of Internet buying, as the proportion of women among online buyers increased 9 percentage points, from 29 percent to 38 percent since last summer. 'Men were undoubtedly the early adopters of Internet commerce, but women have recently emerged as a powerful buying force on the Web. The 9-point increase in the proportion of women purchasing via the Web in such a short period of time is substantial,' notes Jerome Samson, director of Technology and Business Strategy, Nielsen Media Research. 'It is especially important considering that the proportion of women among Internet buyers had been stagnant for nearly two years. Now women are active buyers in all the major product categories.'

Whereas women and men generally purchase the same types of products online, with books and CDs/videos in the top spots and in the same order, gender differences are more visible in Web shopping. Women's top shopping items are clothing (6.9 million shoppers) and books (6.2 million shoppers) while men's top shopping items are cars/car parts (12.6 million shoppers) and computers (9.4 million shoppers).

Consider what Sharon Machlis wrote in *Computerworld* in August 1998:

> The gender cybergap quietly narrowed this summer when the nation's most popular online service, America Online, Inc., found it has more female members (52 percent) than males. That's a staggering change from four years ago when 16 percent of AOL members were female, and yet another sign of women's growing presence on the Net.

Therefore, we have to assume that many of the 750,000 purchasers on AOL represent females, thus proving that the purchasers' gender gap is narrowing.

No wonder that, in aiming to attract female surfers,

Lycos, Inc. has made deals in 1999 with women's content sites, Women.com Networks and iVillage.com in New York. Moreover, the Estee Lauder Company in New York has announced plans for a major electronic commerce site for Clinique™ beauty products. The increase in female Web surfers is now assumed to be good news for electronic commerce sites.

"Women buy three times as much in remote (mail or phone order) clothing purchases than men in traditional channels," says Nicole Vanderbilt, an analyst at Jupiter Communications, Inc. in New York.

"The content is as important as the shopping opportunity," adds Marian Salzman, an analyst at Young & Rubicam, Inc.'s Brand Futures Group in New York. "Commerce is just an extra for them." Women find online communities attractive—not only chat rooms and bulletin boards, but areas such as those developed by Amazon.com for users to write reviews about books they read, Salzman points out.

Web retailers are also trying to develop features that are likely to appeal to women. For example, The Gap, Inc.'s Web site offers "Virtual Style," where men and women can mix and match outfits. This feature is more interesting to women, who care about mixing and matching when shopping in physical stores as well. Appliance maker Whirlpool Corporation relaunched its home page in 1997 after learning the majority of users were women. Internet staffers added more links, useful information, and click-on icons for easier navigation. "You may have been going after the 20- to 30-year-old male, and now your demographics have changed to over half your users being female. Your market is changed, and your Web site has to address the audience appropriately," says Brett Knoblock, Whirlpool's manager of interactive consumer marketing.

However, do women believe all this hype? An e-mail

from the Systers July 1998 listserv reads:

> *I've been disappointed recently by the surprising lack of interest that the big Web sites have in women users. Some of this comes from some recent events here at CNET, including a Snap.com's promotional campaign that focuses on speed and a ride in a Russian MIG. I'm not saying that women shouldn't ride MIGs. I personally think that would be cool. I'm saying that the big search/portal sites seem to be happily ignoring our presence on the Net, and are choosing not to spend their advertising dollars courting us. I think that this is a huge mistake on their part since I expect that traffic from women users has the potential for enormous growth.*

—Susan Dorward
Senior Software Engineer, CNET, Inc.

Women's Concerns—Web or Not

In order to understand how we can reach out and capture the women's market online, we first must acquaint ourselves with market research that focuses on the market segment, such as that published by Women Trend, Inc. in 1997. The company lists the major issues women told them they face in the '90s:

1. Time management
2. Family and work balance
3. Community participation
4. Financial security
5. Health care
6. Fitness and nutrition
7. Education (self and kids)

They also listed current trends in women's lives such as:

- Volatility—tastes and aspirations change constantly
- Family—new definitions emerge
- Mobility—nomad dads, commuter couples, single moms by choice
- Portability—traveling with technology and comfort
- Simplicity—discarding the nonsense of life
- Humanity—renewed focus on others, not self
- Well-being—spiritual, physical, and emotional health
- Technology—being online and alone
- Affinity—clanning with others
- Responsibility—for the environment, government, and children

These trends' imperatives are:

- Time has become the essential focus in a woman's life.
- Health and well-being are now a daily concern.
- Simplicity and balance are sought with conviction.
- The blurring of moral and social boundaries is leading to confusion.
- Cohorts now serve as surrogate families.
- The mantra is: "Follow the kids; they're wired."
- The future to watch for involves mostly education, environment, and aging issues.

A 1997 conference on marketing to women on the Web

by the International Research Institute confirmed the conclusion by Women Trend: Time is the essential focus in a woman's life. Each woman seeks to expand the utility of time through juggling, multitasking, etc. Thirty-eight percent of working mothers cut back on sleep to make more time. All are struggling with fitting everything in—family, career, exercise. The true status symbol is the affordability of leisure time. The majority of women state that lack of time is the main reason for their not using the Internet.

The conference also reported that 48 percent of working mothers say they are under constant stress. According to 60 percent of women, stress is their number one on-the-job problem. Women do not want to increase their stress level by struggling to understand a new technology like the Internet. As long as that technology is not crucial to their daily life, they would rather let others master it first.

Women's Economic Influence

But what companies are waking up to is women's emerging economic clout:

- Their increasing level of education
- Their greater participation in the workforce
- The narrowing wage/salary gap
- Their growing influence in business
- Their entrepreneurial drive
- Their longer life expectancy

And business can no longer ignore these facts:

- Women write 80 percent of all checks.
- Women pay 61 percent of all bills.

- Women own 53 percent of all stocks.
- Women earn 85-90 percent of what men earn.
- Women account for 75 percent of all consumer spending in the U.S.
- Approximately 40 percent of all small businesses in the U.S. are owned by women, and they represent the fastest growing segment of the economy, increasing at twice the rate of all U.S. businesses.

What Women Want from the Net

Therefore, women represent a huge marketing opportunity to those companies who are willing to help them overcome some of the real and perceived barriers to using the Net. For example, women are significantly more likely than men to express being extremely/very concerned about credit card security (90 percent vs. 83 percent) (Lycos, Inc., March 1998 survey). With women being the fastest growing population on the Internet, it is fascinating that many companies have not taken the time to study carefully what women say they seek on the Net. Quality of content is the highest rated feature women are looking for. Second to that is building a relationship. "They'd rather buy a dishwashing liquid with less lemon from a company that sponsors after-school programs," says Faith Popcorn in a 1997 issue of *AdAge*.

Women expect more from a business relationship than men; they want more dialogue, more affinity, and longer time horizons for the relationship to develop. A company can create a brand bond with a woman by emphasizing product quality, relevance, corporate outreach, and consumer affinity—and have an ongoing interaction with her. Furthermore, women want their own virtual communities. Women fully understand how to use the Net as a community. They know the Net is not just about socializing but about problem solving, that on the Net you can handpick your virtual neighbors, use experts, and share everybody's wisdom.

Major themes for women consumers have always been:

- Trust
- Giving value
- Innovation
- Relationships
- Relevance

Therefore, when going online, women are looking for ease of use, simplicity, convenience, dependability, networking, communication, and support. Women want to log on at any time and find relevant information. They view the Net as a tool and want to be shown how best to use it. They want it to improve their knowledge.

In 1997 Women Connection Online, one of the most successful Web sites for women, shared this list of successful strategies in marketing to women online in a regional seminar:

- Partner with complementary communities that have already developed trust with your target audience.
- Use appropriate advertising/sponsorship (pull out immediately what does not work!).
- Offer interactive tools (how much do I need to save for college? retirement?).
- Sell value-added products and services (groceries? flowers?).
- Link with key sites: family, fitness, travel, celebrities, music and movies.

- Create a good balance of information and graphics.
- Offer freebies like coupons, sweepstakes, and ideas.
- Create a virtual community and offer chats with experts and like-minded individuals.
- Create a relationship page that talks about what your company is doing for women and why they understand women's special needs.
- Remember to use your Web site as a platform for your company, one that enables the creation of relationship marketing.

Women's Wire, another prominent site, advised companies attending the seminar to remember that women on the Net are mostly looking for:

- Utility
- Sense of community
- Problem solving
- Getting data and doing something with it

The most popular iVillage site creators shared what they found out:

1. 85 percent of their women audience wanted information on parenting.
2. 50 percent of women wanted information on finance.
3. 50 percent of women wanted information on careers.

AOL's list of women's interest areas in comparison looked like this:

- 60 percent—entertainment
- 58 percent—career
- 55 percent—news
- 53 percent—books
- 51 percent—women's studies

AOL's women users requested pragmatic information, such as:

- How to advance in my career?
- How to chose a fragrance?
- Who should be our role models?
- How to create an affordable wardrobe?
- How to create a meal in 10 minutes?

Aliza Sherman, the creator of the web's first women's site, Cybergrrl, makes these recommendations to those wanting to attract women to their Web site:

- Identify yourself.
- Use a voice that mirrors the community you're trying to build.
- Create a loyal following and let those women give you constant feedback so they feel they have ownership of your content and improvements.
- Respond immediately to suggestions.
- Conduct instant surveys.
- Ask for registration information (if you answer a few questions, you can get in for free) and guarantee that information will not be sold.
- Choose core topics to start with and then let your audience suggest the rest.
- Don't be afraid to give something for free!

- Invite, engage, customize, educate, relate, build trust, provide value, and create relevance.

We can't assume that women and men want the same information, process information the same way, or use words the same. Women have different needs and values, different purchasing behaviors, and different expectations of business relationships. Women's needs center around time, information, and security. Women's values are different. Women see the world differently–they care more about more issues (the environment, global ethics, voluntarism, arts and culture, and opportunities for other women). Men view the world as a hierarchy of leaders and followers. Women see it as a network of relationships and friendships. Men want to be respected. Women want to be liked.

We can reinforce these observations by studying gender differences in computer games usage, as Patricia Pearce documented in her book, *The Interactive Book:*

Males Seek	*Females Seek*
An individual experience	A social experience
Being king of the hill	Creating level ground
Winning	Solving a problem
Ugliness, grotesqueness	Beauty, cuteness
Danger	Safety
Dexterous challenge	Intellectual and emotional challenge
Strategy	Understanding
Advantage	Insight
Team play	Group play
Feedback	Response
Individual activities	Overall context and ambiance
Good vs. evil conflict	Inner life
Human-to-machine interaction	Person-to-person contact

So where do women go on the Net? A NetSmart survey from 1997 ranks the main areas:

1. E-mail
2. Chat/forums
3. News
4. Business and career
5. Parenting and family
6. Personal finance
7. Health and fitness

E-mail to date is still women's favorite activity on the Net. Information is the main draw. Women do not surf! Saving time is part of the equation of buying online.

Web Marketing Strategies for Women

So what should retailers offer to women online? At a 1998 conference on Women and the Web, 1-800-Flowers recommended what they had implemented:

- Offer convenience, replenishment.
- Fill a need, try to provide hard-to-find products.
- Promote a sense of community, of sharing peer information.
- Emphasize user friendliness, ease of use.
- Offer a personal touch, an identity.
- Marry context/content with product .
- Show how to avoid surfing.

On the other hand, Legg's found out that a Web design that appeals to women is one that:

- Is easy and fast to maneuver
- Is innovative
- Is educational
- Makes it easy to dialog with company
- Maintains a constant online dialog

When women using iVillage were asked what would make them shop online, their response was:

- Utility, functionality
- Time savings, a quick process
- Good service, help
- Relevance, personal touch

When asked about women-friendly advertising themes, they wanted to see:

- Women in multiple roles
- Kid-friendly context
- An environmentally friendly message
- Successful, realistic women portrayals
- Women aging in positive ways
- Women as "time challenged," active, busy but coping

An October 1998 *Inc. Magazine* article sums up the overwhelming reasons why marketing to women on the Web is a win-win strategy:

> For those who want to bet on the distant future, Lauren Freedman, president of E-Tailing Group, an electronic commerce consulting and development firm based in Chicago, recommends products for women. As more women gain access to the Internet

(women are still a minority online, making up slightly less than 50 percent of the users), Freedman expects that the online market for women's products, particularly clothes and fashion basics such as pantyhose and cosmetics, will explode. 'If you want to get rich on the Web,' says Freedman, 'you have to start targeting women.'

A *Forbes* magazine article from September 1998 further reinforces this point:

'Until now, women's sites have been underrepresented,' says Richard LeFurgy, chairman of the Internet Advertising Bureau and the FAST Forward Steering Committee. 'That's mainly a function of women lagging as users on the Internet.' The latest findings present what LeFurgy says is "a clarion call" to developers. 'It's time,' he says, 'to aggressively target female demographics via the Web.' Not only are women who use the Web more educated (according to Simmons Market Research, 26 percent of women online hold masters degrees), employed in greater numbers (85 percent are employed), and wealthier than their offline female cohorts (62 percent report an annual household income of more than $50,000), they are responsible for 70-90 percent of the buying decisions within a household.

'When you unleash that kind of purchasing power over the Web,' says Marleen McDaniel, CEO of California-based Women.com, 'the implications are huge.' McDaniel's privately held network of six sites generates 30 million page views monthly. And she asserts that in the emerging Web economy, women replace men as the primary focus of commercial activity. Women on the Web are the next major marketing niche.

Chapter 4

Building a Web Site for Women

Women's presence on the Web has grown immensely from only 5 percent of users in 1994 to 48 percent in 1999. The main reasons women are online are:

1. Convenience—they want to simplify their lives.
2. Information—they want information that helps them get things done and make the right buying decisions.
3. The ability to solve problems—they seek frequent involvement and interaction.

When experts are asked, "What do women want from the Web?" their answer invariably is "convenience, utility, and more time." If a woman makes it to your site, she has already shown strong interest in you, so you need to take that under consideration. You need to use her presence to strengthen your brand recognition.

If you are the content provider, what kind of content can you reasonably and reliably offer? Clinique™ chose to be a content provider on the Web beyond just selling cosmetics. They have developed a woman's guide to the Web as well as cover women's issues on their site. Women trust that content because they trust the quality of the Clinique™ brand.

To reach women, a site must develop *trust*. It is the number one issue with women. How are you going to win their trust? Be up-front with what you're doing, let them know where the content comes from—if it's a commercial entity or an expert. Let them know what you will do with the information you gather from them.

The average age of women on the Web is 38. It is the sandwich generation, so these women are very busy. They go online less frequently than men. A mean session of a woman is 48 minutes compared to a man's 67 minutes session.

Women are more selective and are lighter users than men; they are most interested in sites and applications dedicated to specific content and communication. Women want utility from the Web. They want something that works and do not care how it works! They do not need to bang their hands against technology. They want to get specific information or shop.

Checklist for Reaching Women on the Web

1. In building a site for women, get to know your specific female audience first. Each generation of users has different needs:

    • *Generation Y* (young women 15-25 years old) wants instant gratification. The emphasis is on making friends on the Web, meeting people their age, looking for teens with similar interests. Teen girls are chatting online in huge numbers. They do not use e-mail lists as much as other generations. They love surveys and quizzes. They love to enter contests, e-mail, build personal Web sites, get expert advice, and use chat rooms, instant messaging and AOL buddy lists.

- *Generation Xers* (women 25-40 years old) want useful and entertaining information and self-expression. They e-mail a lot and do a lot of information gathering. They prefer lists to posting boards. They talk about everything. They are already making purchases online. They like how-to's, e-mail lists, search engines, and the like.

- *Boomers* (women 40-55 years old) want valuable information. They will interact for a purpose. They are making purchases online, but they are also information gatherers. E-mail is very big with them. Their surfing is more directed and specific—"can I use it?" They like to do research and seek in-depth information that is reliable. They like to use searchable databases.

2. Women of different ages also seek different experiences on the Web. Make sure you know how to reach each group:

   - Women in their 20s—try to capture their interests.
   - Women in their 30s—realize they are transitioning their lives, building families, etc.
   - Women in their 40s—have the discretionary funds to spend.

Remember you also need to give all these women what they still don't know they need! That's why you need to keep your site very organic.

3. Do you need editors on your staff? Partner with people who are in the business of writing. On the Web "the community is the content," and this fact can be a big liability and cause fear for a lot of big companies. However, many companies have worked out the legal terms to make it happen Women are making connections online with people and with content. Once women place something on a site (participate in a chat, for instance)–they are compelled to return.

4. Whose voice is on your site? Do you have a personality to represent you? If you use surveys, let the results be things that women can use (i.e., questions about food will get them back diet tips). Your privacy policy should be at the bottom of every page on your site.

5. An e-mail newsletter can remind people what is on the Web site. It allows you to go into your users' personal space, so you have to be respectful of it. You must get permission!

6. "My site"—customizing and personalizing content—requires a lot of technology. Therefore, you might need technology partners to make it happen. You can also use syndicated content (like the National Cancer Society content about breast cancer which is available free) and post it on your site to add value to your site.

How to market to women on the Web

Here is additional expert advise shared by participants at the August 1999 "Marketing to Women on the Web" International Research Institute conference in New York City:

1. Since women are making a lot of the decisions about bringing things into the family, into the home, trust is a big issue with them. And the Net is still a questionable medium. You do not want them to lose their feeling of comfort. E-mail is more private than your physical mailbox, so there is greater sensitivity as to what you receive in your e-mail box.

2. Word-of-mouth is the dominant way women find out about sites. The search engines that women use a lot are looksmart.com and askjeeves. Women also use women's magazines to link into other Web sites.

3. As for chat rooms, women make lateral connections; they want to chat and they use the Web to stay connected. However, women in their 30s and 40s use chat, but only when it is scheduled.

4. Always give your Web consumer another option for buying–go to the store, get a catalog, etc.

5. When building a new site, separate the site by lifestyle That will allow for more real-life shopping experience. Allow for multiple ways to navigate the site.

6. With one click women should be able to buy your

product. Do not waste their time with content if all they want is to buy! They want access to the data, but not to have it stand in their way.

7. You have to change the site all the time to maintain traffic. Bring something different to the top of the Web page all the time.

8. Women love experts to ask questions of. If you help them, their appreciation carries over into buying.

9. When you build an e-commerce site, you must have commitment. You must answer your consumer's needs all the time. You must have the human resources and budget to meet those needs.

10. High-touch fashion requires strong and full imagery. Even if the images take longer to load, use them.

11. Minimize friction on your site. Make the initial services free and light.

12. Reward women for talking; flatter them for talking.

13. Be approachable; put your URL everywhere; make it easy to pass it on; give away your site.

14. Build fun or usefulness or incentive with every interaction.

15. For traffic building, use search engines, packaging, publicity, advertising, and viral marketing.

Myths about women on the Web

Besides these proactive design characteristics, there are some myths you need to avoid when designing your site:

1. *"Women do not care about the technology."* Women may not care about how it works, but they do care that it DOES work!

2. *"Women want and trust men to control the e-commerce decision."*
   Women are the gatekeepers for health on behalf of their entire family. You need to address relevant issues that apply not just to them but to everyone else as well.

3. *"You only need one message for women."* Women's needs are very diverse, so use the medium to its fullest extent. The home page should quickly direct a user towards her area of interest; the banners also need to direct her to those areas.

4. *"Women take a slow methodical approach to the Web."*
   Women do not have time to waste. They want fast and easy access. Women are not window-shopping and impulse-buying; they are making largely planned purchases. They know what they want, and they want to get it fast.

5. *"Women want a serious approach to serious subjects."*
   You need to touch women's emotions, and they appreciate a sense of humor. You want to use a tone of voice that is honest and light that allows you to bond

with the customer and create a relationship.

6. *"Women will tolerate and deal well with traffic jams."*
Women will turn off a site when they feel too many
conflicting messages are being thrust at them at once.
Make information specific and consistent.

7. *"Women do not bond with complicated things."*
Women want to find sites they can fully trust and
be loyal too. Also women want to know that you
appreciate their business. Customer service and communication are critical.

8. *"Women are comfortable with things they know."*
Women reward creativity. Delight them with something special. Show them you are thinking about
them in ways they have not seen before.

Build Your Web Site to Attract Women

Here are the 10 steps to building your Web site to appeal to women as recommended by Ellen Reid Smith, a well-
known Internet consultant:

1. Establish marketing goals and objectives.

Ask yourself: what is the purpose for my Web site? What is it
I want to happen at the end of the day? Be honest and specific.
Objectives such as relationship building, reaching new audiences,
offering a different product, extending an existing product, and
providing better service and support are examples. The goal needs
to be driven from the top of your organization. You can have mul-

tiple goals—you can be focusing on branding and then build relationships with only your most loyal customers. Make sure you have measurable objectives; how will you know you have succeeded? Is your success more about sales or brand awareness? Measurements can be things such as total new customers, new customers in targeted audiences, customer satisfaction, and the like.

2. Define scale and budget.

Planning can be circular, and you might need to go through several rounds before you decide how to pay for your Web site development. The frequency of content update is a huge budget driver, also how much electronic commerce you are going to do. Other factors are the degree of customer interaction on the site, personalization of the content, and the breadth of your product line. Deciding on these is very important to do early! Outsourcing versus in-house development is a cost driver as well.

The average development time for a site is one year. Electronic commerce sites are high cost—sometimes higher than content-driven ones. One million is an average expense for an extensive electronic commerce site. Remember that labor is the biggest cost. And cost for labor will continue to increase as long as there is a shortage of skilled designers and developers.

3. Define your female target audience based on value.

There are three typical customer segmentations: product-based, demographics-based, and psychographic-based. However, your best bet is not to ask the customer what she wants to buy—but ask her who she is, and then tell her what you have for her. You need to identify your best customer, your most valuable customer, and find out what she has been buying in the last two years and for how much. Get as much data about her habits, likes, and dislikes as you can. Find out how much she is going to spend and then offer her different types of bargains. Every product is different, so you need to do this for every category you offer.

You can also purchase a "generic customer profile" if you cannot create your own model. Your site should be built to match the profile and meet the needs of the woman who owns that profile. Retention, click-through, or frequency then becomes the means to increase the lifetime value of the site. Therefore, your Web site should be designed NOT for the average customer but rather your BEST customer! You also need to design for "potentials", the customers who have the potential to become your best customers.

4. Develop a Web strategy and design.

You must match the style, the habits, the status, and everything else that fits your customer's style. Make sure you constantly thank your best customers for doing business with you. Decide what are you offering:

- virtual newsstand offering magazine titles
- channel-based system that makes navigation easy
- community, shopping, and service to make the Web fun and productive
- established Web brands at your fingertip

5. Build relationships to keep women coming. Your measurements for building a relationship should be:

- "stickiness" —time spent on site per visit
- relationships—value-based exchange
- loyalty—being blind to competitors.

Demonstrate the value to your customer; answer the question, "What am I going to get for being loyal?" Build trust by being brutally honest about what the relationship will be about. Tell them about the benefits they are going to get (what special discounts, what free information, what points can you collect). Package the benefits into a program or a club. Furthermore, guaranty privacy and demonstrate you can be trusted. Always ask permission to have a relationship. Separate registration on the site from receiving the newsletter; make them EARN the right to be a member.

State all requirements and benefits up front (you need to spend that much to remain a member). Elevate the conversation to an intelligent dialog–the Web is beautiful for this because it can track the whole exchange. Let the audience know that tracking their moves will allow you to make the site better for them and give them more and more value. You need to remember to reward women for giving you information on a regular basis–every time they answer a quiz, sign up for something, update their profile, etc. The reward for loyalty can be done through discounts, service, entertainment, community, access, point program, games/sweeps, or information/advice. Remember: Customers are not equal and should NOT be treated equally, so vary your awards. Keep working on the relationships–develop measurements of retention and defection. Take customer feedback seriously!

6. Achieve woman-to-woman marketing through personalization.

At the very minimum you must speak to your customers like women. The content has to be appealing. Feature women in photos so they can relate to your site. Design for women's preferences by testing your banners, for example. When linking from a women's site to your site, do not drop your customers by all of a sudden changing the tone to too male-oriented. Strive for customization; let the customer choose the content. Knowing what information to collect is very critical—how does your customer make the decision to buy? What solutions do you offer to her? Do not, however, bombard your online customer with questions and thus spoil the relationship. Use maybe an online panel of most valued customers and let them answer a lot of questions for a reward. You must create trust before asking questions that are too personal.

7. Acquire strategic partners.

If you do not want to develop your own Web site, look to those partners who already reach the audience you want to reach. A partner strategy should enhance your product and the experience of this product. Also your partners need to help you gain credibility. There are products that women have learned to trust, so use them to drive traffic to your site. Look and see who your competition partners with. Develop the vehicle for attracting partners—what is the value proposition for the partner? What techniques are you going to use to promote the partner? You are selling opportunities for your partner, not just advertising. Create joint marketing opportunities. And reserve the best opportunities for the partners (vs. advertisers). Determine who pays whom. Make it a win-win. Partnering should be for a minimum of a year because it takes a long time to create the partnership presence. Make sure you have a "cafeteria" of opportunities to fit different size partners. But remember, you need to value your site and your customers enough not to give anything away to a partner!

8. Integrate your site.

Integrate a women's area into the mass market Web site by separating the content or putting it deep inside any other areas. For integrating the Web into overall marketing, use advertising, product design, and so forth. Sponsor events, get public relations coverage, submit your site to women-rated sites, and get endorsements.

9. Attract women to your site.

You must know what you expect and how you will measure it. Then decide on the best techniques like site style, historical response rates, context, and offline awareness building. Design does make a difference. Create interaction through games or quizzes, but remember that a customer will leave a page after 5-7 seconds if the page does not load! Never underestimate the importance of relevance: seasonal relevance, prize relevance, or partner relevance.

How will you measure your ROI? Use measurements like:

- Building a successful relationship via community
- Increased sales
- Lower costs of lead generation
- Maximizing efficiency
- Providing more efficient information
- Strengthening your distribution channel

You have to have metrics because the opportunity is huge! Count the number of consumers requesting a branded product or the number of visitors who leave data or the number of consumers who return a feedback form. For your media campaign, know that the Net is a $2 investment per person (or lead) versus other media (TV is $36). And that goes down every time the consumer revisits a site (if they come back at least three times, they become free visitors as long as the Web site delivers).

Do not duplicate what you're doing in other media on your Web site. Become a 24-hour interactive environment or make it commerce-related. That way you know you are adding value.

Designing a Web Site for Women

As for the design of the Web site itself, here are a few recommendations from the designers at women.com:

- Your site's look and feel should appeal to women. For example, straight lines do not work as well as curves.
- Women like pastel colors and softness. Black and red are considered very male. Yellow is female.
- The "voice" of your site has to be right, not harsh.
- Always, always ask your customer what she thinks— use focus groups, observe women interact with your site, conduct online surveys.
- Let the women help you design the site. The profile of the woman on the Web has really morphed, so pay attention to that and do not assume the answer is the same as last year!

To summarize, an *Internet World* article from August 1999, "Effectively Reaching Women on Line," gave the following advice:

- Stress ease of navigation and use
- Emphasize contextual selling
- Use transactive content
- Offer personalization
- Provide best-of-class customer service

Women online are a separate niche market. If you understand what they want and give it to them, they will reward you with loyalty, valuable feedback, and invigorating community—and maybe even a healthy profit.

Chapter 5

Powerful Web Women: Our New Role Models and Their Stories

Deb Triant
CEO , Check Point, Inc.
Summer 1998
www.checkpoint.com

Even as women are discovering their compatibility with the Web, key women have already made an impact in the Internet arena. Deb Triant certainly qualifies as one. She is one of the few women CEOs in Silicon Valley and was featured this year on the cover of *Fortune* magazine as the CEO of one of the "coolest" new high-tech companies in the U.S. During the 1998 Women in Technology International Conference, Deb Triant rejoiced, "The Internet provides an unprecedented opportunity for women to get to the top jobs. It creates a level of opportunity that was never there before for a significant number of women. The Internet is 'sucking up' new talent; it is no longer a 'nerdy technology.' It is about new ways of marketing, reading customers…. The creative side is ruling. You can create businesses in any line."

Deb Triant grew up in California. She has a Ph.D. in mathematics from Columbia University. She was picked as

Check Point's CEO while working at Adobe as a vice president of marketing. Check Point is an Israeli company which produces firewall software. Deb is responsible for making it a market leader in less than two years. Check Point's 1997 revenues were $100 million. Its market valuation, though, is $1.2 billion.

When I met Deb Triant on a particularly hot day in Dallas, she was extremely friendly and forthcoming. When she heard about my book writing, she immediately whipped out from her bag the book, *Sex on the Brain,* by Deborah Bloom and started quoting passages from it. She made sure I understood that she agreed wholly with the book's premise that there are definite differences between men and women. She elaborated on how the female style of management thrives on teamwork, networking, and support and not "testosterone-driven competition."

She told me she felt very lucky to have arrived at Silicon Valley as an executive at a time when everything is moving so fast that organizations cannot use rigid hierarchical structures and have to adopt more female-oriented organic modes of growth. "That is why," she said, "women are now starting to really make it in the Valley. The faster change occurs, the better women's flexible style of management works."

When asked about the Web, she exclaimed, "The Web is not only a tool that is complementary of women's style of management and communication. It is also a faster way to communicate, more immediate, and therefore it appeals more to women who do not get hung up on rigid structures."

Deb went on to tell me that when she manages, unlike a man, she does not feel she has to know it all. "I need to know that you know very well that which I do not know," she explained. She is happy to be "the" expert in her area of specialty–marketing. At Check Point, she has an open door policy and tells all of her employees to feel free to come in and tell her about their work and problems.

On the issue of web-like networking, she commented, "We women like to create networks that are the fibers from which our lives are made. We accept other women as equal contributors to the network. We are not driven to establish a pecking order." On the other hand, because women expect equality from their co-networkers, they do not take lightly to being "stabbed in the back" by other women. Men, on the other hand, will stab another man in the back while working and then go out and have a beer with him. Men believe that the work environment is based on competition and all is fair in "love and war." Once they leave that environment, they can act differently. "If you stab me in the back, " said Deb Triant, "I am not likely to forget it so fast or consider it only part of being competitive."

Deb is not sure that women's and men's working styles can be meshed together to create a perfect work environment. She understands why many women have chosen to quit and start their own businesses rather than try and find a solution to that problem. She sums up the gender differences by saying, "If a man hears a woman CEO saying, 'I could not have done this without my team,' he considers it as a display of weakness. How come she could not have done it herself as a true leader?"

Deb Triant is definitely a leader, but she also is a real team player. She has been called "the biggest factor in Check Point's success" and "the 50 million dollar lady." She does not consider herself the "biggest factor in Check Point's success." Rather, she claims, "Yes, I am a critical factor in its success. That is not to say that I am the only factor, but they could not have done it without my contribution."

As Deb Triant hurried to get on one more flight, she commented happily about getting ready to take two weeks off for her honeymoon. With a big smile on her face, she truly seemed like just "one of the girls." And, boy, do we need more girls like her!

Jacquie Winder
Founder, Women's Web in Australia
August 1999
www.womensweb.org.au

Women's Web is designed to assist women to learn about the Internet by using a mentoring model. From Wodonga across northern Victoria to Swan Hill and beyond, local women acting as teachers and mentors assist and support others through the process of learning. Through the program a thousand women are to be trained in the first year in basic Internet skills. This training will take place in local schools, neighborhood houses, adult and community education centers, and other community venues.

The Women's Web project aims to:

- give women the training and self-confidence to use the Internet to access information relevant to their lives.
- increase the skills of women, enabling them to mentor others.
- train at least 1,000 women in basic Internet skills in the first 12 months.
- identify local points of access for women and promote their use.
- provide a forum for rural women to communicate

with each other through electronic mailing lists and the Women's Web site.

- develop further training opportunities for women to enhance their Internet skills if desired.

An example of how the project works is Jennifer, who was not at all interested in the Internet. As far as she was concerned, it was for teenage boys with nothing to do except play games and look for dirty pictures. She had a property to run! Her friend Kathy knew she was going to have an uphill battle convincing her to come along to a Women's Web training session that was being held at the local primary school. Kathy was certain that being able to access stock and commodity prices, up-to-date weather information, and animal care information would interest Jennifer.

The truth was Jennifer didn't like computers. She was scared even to turn one on, fearing she would break it! So Kathy convinced her that if she came along, she didn't have to touch it; she could just watch while Kathy operated the computer.

So as a pair Kathy and Jennifer went along to the class and were shown how to use a browser to look for Web sites about agricultural and rural interests and how to access the latest rural news and weather information. Using e-mail, they joined an e-mail discussion list that had many other farmers in Jennifer's area sending each other information and assistance. Jennifer was hooked—so much to see! She was still worried about using a computer, but now she had a reason to learn and, with the help of her mentor who supported Jennifer when she felt unsure, she was able to use the Internet without being aware that she was in fact using a computer. While finding her feet, Jennifer accessed the Internet through her local primary school after-hours at a time arranged for Women's Web members to gain access. Here she was able to get help from other women using the Internet and from her mentor, who was able to drop by on occasion to help.

Kathy was very pleased that Jennifer was able to gain more confidence using a computer and the Internet and was pleased that she too could now use the Internet to further her own interest in medicinal herbs. She also discovered that she could get Web space that would enable her to develop her own Web page. She could now publish the information she had discovered on herbal remedies and growing herbs to share with others with her interest. She has joined mailing lists run by others with an interest in herbal remedies and regularly chats with others around the world. Jacquie Winder got the idea for the Women's Web Project from a project developed by the Queensland University of Technology that gave rural and isolated women in outback Queensland computers and modems to explore how communication technologies could assist them.

Although somewhat different in focus, Jacquie's project sought funding from Skills.net, a statewide project that funds community organizations to train and give Internet access to everyone in the state of Victoria. Women's Web was designed to fit those project guidelines although it covers northern Victoria.

While developing the project, Jacquie brought together a wide range of rural women and representatives of rural women's interest groups to discuss the project and the ways in which it could best be made to fit the needs and interests of rural women in Victoria. It was at this meeting that the project really took shape with the input of both experienced Internet users and the "I've never touched a computer in my life" women.

Jacquie herself began using the Internet in 1995 while

working in a local computer shop. Customers began to ask about this Internet "thing," and the technician and Jacquie decided to learn about this Internet "thing" so they could talk to their customers about it. Besides having a new "geeky" thing to play with, they convinced the manager to get the shop connected. It was quite expensive then, as it still is by comparison with city areas, but they soon realized that their wonderful tool was more than just fun and games. They could download software—drivers and patches and updates; look up technical databases and manufacturers' information; and much more. This doesn't seem like such a big deal now, but it was then. It was just so useful and so interesting, and they could communicate with all sorts of people all over the world.

As soon as an Internet service provider organized a point of connection to the Internet within local calling access to where she was living (30kms away from town), Jacquie herself got connected and used the Internet mainly for study, but she certainly had more than a few late nights e-mailing, chatting, and surfing. Having a fine arts background, she had been into computer-generated art for a while, and so she soon became interested in Web page design and construction. More recently, the social and educational aspects of Internet use have interested her, and she has begun a masters degree looking at the gender aspects of online learning.

The project has finished its first phase, which is preparing the women selected and specially trained by Women's Web to mentor and teach women from their local area. Mentors are currently out training and supporting other women and using computers in community settings or in their own homes. The mentors have access to a bank of laptops, and these have been invaluable in getting training and access to isolated communities. The project designers are getting lots of positive feedback, and after their training, some mentors have gone on to obtain employment as computer tutors. This was one of the reasons Jacquie made sure that the mentor training was accredited.

Knowing the current status of women using the Net in Australia is difficult because every set of statistics is different. One late set had Australian women just ahead of the U.S. at about 43 percent of women using the Internet. This of course would not be true in rural areas. Other studies quote figures such as 27 percent and some even lower. Regardless of the actual usage figures, Women's Web has been a factor for social change. Jacquie said, "Employment for some of the project participants has been one successful outcome—especially with such a high unemployment rate in rural areas. The use of the Internet and computers by women on farms certainly has produced some quite radical changes in farm practice and management in terms of up-to-date information about weather, pricing, and the buying and selling of goods and produce online. Women seem to enjoy e-mail in particular, and this ability to communicate with others even though they may be physically isolated is certainly a major drawing card for women to learn about the Internet. We have trained women who were quite adamant about their refusal to learn about computers or the Net—until a son or daughter went interstate or overseas and handed them an e-mail address!"

Jacquie is hopeful that the project will go statewide sometime next year. The Office of Women's Affairs is behind the project and is doing all they can to help expand its scope. Finding other "geekgirls" has not been easy in rural Australia, but Jacquie keeps up with the geekboys she used to know when she worked at the computer shop. "Women's Web has certainly widened the circle of women I know involved in this field, however," she added.

The Net has also enabled her to continue studying at a university many, many miles away without leaving the house. "This will be such a great thing for rural communities when online learning finally finds its feet," Jacquie predicted. "I do all my banking and bill paying online (I HATE spending lunchtimes paying bills and waiting in bank queues), and I use the Net for holiday information and bookings, looking for events, helping the kids with homework, and finding maps to places I'm travelling to. It's about the only way I keep in touch with some of my friends. I don't know what I'd do without it!"

The main change she would like to see in the Internet is more speed. In rural areas the Net can be really slow at times. "I would really like something to happen in regards to the pornography and pedophilia that is so rampant," she stated, "but I also feel strongly about freedom of speech, so I'm not sure about that. I find it really offensive and it is certainly a BIG deterrent for women to come online. I would like the Net (and computing in general, I guess) to become less "Bill Gates-centric," and I also hope that it doesn't get any more clogged with advertising and junk than it already is." She also would like affordable Internet access for everyone—and not just Western countries—and much more interactivity. "Edward de Bono has some interesting views about the Internet and thinking," Jacquie said, "and to use the Internet as a tool/medium for real and positive social change for everyone in this way would be the most wonderful thing it could do."

Doris Booth
Creator and owner , Authorlink!
October 1998
www.authorlink.com

Welcome to Authorlink!, a unique online infor-
mation service for writers, editors, literary agents
and publishers. We showcase, market and match
quality manuscripts to fit publishers' specific needs.
An award-winning news, information, and mar-
keting service for editors, literary agents and writ-
ers. Now more than 125,000 loyal readers a year!

Doris Booth is the creator/founder and CEO of Authorlink!, the first online business to help authors link with potential publishers and agents. As such, the company takes advantage of a business model that has become very successful on the Internet-the online mediator. For a reasonable subscription price, Authorlink! allows authors to showcase samples of their work to the whole publishing community for the purpose of landing a publishing deal.

Doris Booth is a visionary. She is helping transform the business of marketing new works by gathering the best of the Internet characteristics of community, efficiency, and inclusivity.

The idea for Authorlink! was born at a workshop. As she listened to some authors read their manuscripts, Doris wondered, "Why aren't they getting published?" They have no marketing experience, she concluded. Her background in journalism, interactive multimedia production, and publishing helped her devise a solution to the problem. "I recognized the way the technology was moving," she said, "because I had worked with software companies and knew the Internet represented the future of technology. I decided that writers needed to use this medium to their advantage, as their marketing tool."

In early 1980s Doris had become involved in interactive multimedia and she had the big "aha" then about digital technology enabling people to search through huge amounts of data quickly—to compress learning time. Working with CD-ROM technology, she realized that CDs are not an entertainment device, just a delivery device. She knew that as a society we needed a better way to deliver interactive information using a medium that was not too hard to use. And that medium became the Internet because it is free of much of the expense of using a hard medium like CDs, but it can still deliver multimedia. As she did a lot of interface design in multimedia, she realized the Web's potential immediately.

However, Doris had to learn on her own. All she had was three weeks of training at the school for interactive design. In the early '80s nobody knew where to get an education in multimedia. Her father was an inventor, so he was a visionary, and that helped her always to think about the "what if's" and look at the leading edge of things. Her mother was an artist, so she also dreamed about the future and gave Doris permission to do that too.

As vice president of the International Interactive Communication Society, Doris used to sit at some of the big standards meetings and realized even then that companies had to get the technology down to something everyone can understand. "Technology for technology's sake is not enough," Doris thought. "We have to see it for the good of humanity. For example, in the old days writers were very isolated. Now on the Net, they can communicate and therefore avoid some of the scams that have been prevalent; this can empower us as a group."

The Net has helped everyone's ability to communicate; women, being more language-oriented, will benefit from it a lot, Doris believes. The emergence of the Net has offered women a tremendous opportunity to use their interpersonal skills and apply them to a technological base. "However, we need role models." Doris remembers recognizing an early role model: "When I took my first computer skills workshop, there was a woman instructor at the workshop who was all over the floor plugging things into the sockets. It is then that I decided I wanted to do it just like her!"

At seminars across the country Doris does just that as she applies her technology know-how to the publishing industry. She sees gradual change already and is optimistic about further appreciation. She explains, "There is a learning curve we will all have to go through. Two and half years ago editors did not have computers; that has changed immensely. We now have a lot of young editors, and they definitely know how to use computers in the office or at home. I believe that publishers will have to learn how to make the Net a part of their work. The slush piles are killing them; they cannot process the information they get. They need to find a way to be more efficient. Many of them are not as backward anymore; they are very aware that they will have to incorporate technology into their daily business. The business model will evolve to have information channels assist them in organizing publishing information and accessing it as well."

She urges other women to seek innovative ways to use and even design their own Web strategies. "Women should not be afraid. Remember you're a human being first and a woman second. It is how you use your potential that counts!" She stresses that good education, like computer communication skills, is critical. Communication skills as a whole are very important—if you can't speak the language in a foreign country, you won't make it. "We need to use technology to our advantage," she says. "I have seen so much technology hyped up, and that's not where it is either. We need to look for practical ways to solve practical problems."

Doris says success for Web sites depends on staying in a market niche, finding something people need and want, providing "outrageous customer service," and marketing the heck out of the site. She predicts the Internet will be an integral part of our lives from now on. "It allowed me to be in touch with many creative people, which is what I truly love," she says gratefully.

Katharine de Baun
Founder, Moms Online
August 1999
www.momsonline.com

Katharine de Baun is cofounder of Moms Online, the first cyber community for women to become an instant success. She was an English instructor and doctoral student in comparative literature who might have ended up running an espresso stand in Seattle had she not unexpectedly become Alex's mom and an enthusiastic AOL devotee in 1994. And now she states, "This is my calling. My whole life has led me up to this point!"

From the very beginning, Katharine considered Moms Online a long shot. She said, "I was a part-time community college teacher who stopped working just before giving birth to my first child. One afternoon while my baby, Alex, was napping, I was feeling lonely and isolated. Out of boredom, I turned on AOL to see if I had any mail. 'Hey,' I thought, 'I bet they have a Mom's Club on here! Wouldn't that be great?' When I typed in 'Keyword: Mom;' however, I was disappointed. Nothing. Maybe I had the wrong search word? I tried 'mother,' 'maternity,' 'motherhood.' Nothing! I was shocked. There must be something!" Out of her personal disappointment that afternoon came the idea for Moms Online.

The site was a success before many other online communities started emerging. Katharine attributes that success to great distribution on AOL in the early days when they used to give stuff away and actually PAID people to provide content on the service. But, more importantly, there has always been a real spirit and a loving, fun mission behind Moms Online (MO) that is very contagious. "We really DO mean what we say; we have rough edges; we invite people in and let them shape who we become tomorrow," Katharine explained. "Also we have such a fantastically targeted audience—moms who ALWAYS have something to talk about and care passionately about what they do as parents."

Katharine concedes that part of the success of MO is because it is a community run by and for women. The overnight success, however, was not a surprise. "It's strange," Katharine admitted, "but when I got the idea for Moms Online (from looking at the Motley Fool on AOL and then being inspired by new parenthood myself), it almost felt like a gift from on high. I'm not a religious person, but I remember walking around Green Lake in Seattle with my son, Alex, in a stroller, my mind just rolling with enthusiasm as if I'd been shot by an angel. I am quite a cynic about new prospects, but I just KNEW this would work. And when I got anxious with the first proposal to AOL Greenhouse, I had a great dream that helped out. I was sitting at a dining room table, stressing out over

Moms Online, and the ceiling opened up and a great voice boomed, "Just don't care!"—meaning that whatever was going to happen was going to happen and I should enjoy the ride. I feel very, very privileged and grateful to have channeled the birth of Moms Online."

Initially Katharine had no money to do market research, so the site content was based on her very rudimentary exploration of the few message boards that existed on AOL at the time for parenting, her experience of the Motley Fool, and her own hunches and experiences of being a mom.

From day one she could intuitively grasp the potential power of the Internet for parenting. She understood immediately how powerful it could be—especially for new moms who are often isolated just as they are going through the pressure of a huge identity change, not to mention physical changes after birth.

She finds the community of women at MO to be diverse. Some come just to seek information or to read; some come to be entertained; most come for the community. "The online medium is ideal for sharing parenting and personal dilemmas, for reaching out to other women, and for creating virtual coffee klatches," Katharine said.

"The initial feedback about the site was very positive—what surprised us the most was the community, especially chat. Within just a few short weeks there were volunteers banging on the door, wanting to host chats! We had a very impressive array of chats in a short period of time. I think this was key to our success—we were able to create a low-budget cyberplace that was porous enough to invite the audience in. Basically we said, 'This is *yours*! Come on in and make yourself at home. Help us grow.' And it worked!"

Moms Online started in 1996 with seed funding from the AOL Greenhouse, and six months later a second round. They also received revenues from AOL at that point whenever a user spent time in MO—but all this changed suddenly when AOL went to an unlimited service plan and gradually started charging content providers to be on the service (instead of paying them—a complete reversal). Their dependable revenue stream began to trickle, and they struggled to replace it with ad revenues. They were in a weak position for a long time, despite their success. They were on the street looking for investors/buyers because basically they were headed for bankruptcy every week. Many potential investors, however, were scared off by AOL's minority stake in the company. AOL Studios was very close to buying MO at one point, but then that blew up.

"We were like a flea riding on the back of a giant wolf," Katharine remembered. "Then, along came Oxygen. Thank God. Oxygen was like a dream come true, an unbelievable miracle. What could be a better company to buy MO and shepherd it to a great future?" While Moms Online is a commercial entity, it definitely began with mixed motives on Katharine's part. "I tend to lead with an idealistic foot," she explained, "—and hope that the money will follow. I think that this idealistic, sometimes overzealous, spirit at the origins of the company also attracted staff who were similarly inspired and who might have preferred working for a nonprofit cause, and this affected the whole gestalt of the company. Also remember that we 'grew up' in the shelter of the AOL Greenhouse at a time where it was all 'rah, rah, go content!'—and we felt like such a darling. Looking back, we were spoiled. It took us a long time to understand that we WERE a business—and that we had better make money or else. . . . I am very grateful that my brother, Rob, was a cofounder because finances were definitely his strength." Katharine's role in the company evolved over the years.

She spent the first two to three years as editor-in-chief,

managing the whole content and community staff. Then she got pregnant with Beyla during a real drought period for the company. They were just hanging on, month to month, riding on the latest news from AOL, laying off staff, searching for funding with no luck. Katharine cut way back on her role when her second child was born, thinking that once the company was sold she would probably back out entirely.

"I was afraid that MO would be bought by a company on the cheap, a company that would bode ill for its future. But then along came Oxygen, and I started getting ambitious all over again. What an incredible opportunity for MO and for women. I met Gerry Laybourne and decided to move east. I started working full-time again in December on the management team and producing a new area of MO called 'Dare I Say It?' My brother is going to be leaving MO to start a new branch of Oxygen, and a good friend of mine from high school is going to take over as executive producer. I am going to be MO's creative director—which in many ways is the same editor-in-chief role I used to play. Only now MO is so much bigger! I am very excited because now at last we have the resources to make MO really shine in ways that it really needs to to stay afloat."

As the Web has evolved, Katharine doesn't see any huge changes in the way people use the Web—just the volume and pace of communication, more of an e-mail culture, and more of the average person's family and friends online. "I am not really an expert on gender differences on the Web, but I would say that women are more loyal and look for 'homes' more than men do." When referred to as a role model Web entrepreneur, she laughed, "I'm proud of Moms Online and what I started, but I can't quite wrap the words 'role model Web entrepreneur' around myself without feeling a bit silly." Her dreams for the Internet are simple. "I want it to live up to its democratic potential!" she says without hesitation.

Katharine hopes that Moms Online will provide a true service and support for moms everywhere. "They deserve the best!" she insists. In her wildest dreams Katharine fantasizes about moms around the world joining forces to put an end to war, famine, and menstrual cramps.

Rachel Muir
Executive director, Smartgrrls
June 1999
www.smartgrrls.org

We believe that every girl is capable of heroic achievement; that the advancement and innovation of our world is incomplete without women and girls as full partners. We believe in girls making life choices free of boundaries and limits. We promote equal opportunities and equal expectations for girls.

She paddled to the meeting on her bike, with her laptop, PalmPilot, and cellular phone hanging out of her bike's basket. She made a lovely vision of the new millennium's woman executive. She displayed a broad smile and a sweet disposition. Following her was a film crew listening to her every word. They were making a film about an organization she founded called Smartgrrls. The film will enable others to simulate Rachel's dream.

"One thing I have learned is that integrity is expensive," she said. "If you want to do things your way, you should be willing to give it all." Rachel is an outstanding young woman. In two years' time, she has been able to propel an idea she had while in college into a national phenomenon. She is the executive director of Smartgrrls, a non-profit organization dedicated to encouraging girls in math, science, engineering, and technology through hands-on activities and role models. Rachel has single-handedly undertaken the creation of the organization, the solicitation of funds, the establishment of new programs, and the launching of a Web site. She has only two on her staff and relies on volunteers to assist with the growing number of responsibilities for the organization.

I met Rachel via e-mail after my daughter volunteered to work for Smartgrrls. My daughter, who is 22, kept telling me how impressed she was that Rachel, being only four years older than herself, has already accomplished so much. When I finally met Rachel in person, I was struck by how young she is. But very quickly her age no longer was an issue. When I saw her in action talking to her "girls" who were attending the first-ever Smartgrrls summer camp at the University of Texas at Austin, I realized she is a true executive. At the summer camp meeting Rachel exuded confidence and charm. She was fully in charge and talked like a leader. In spite of her casual summer dress and sandals, she commanded the girls' attention and respect. She was the "girl-boss" and they all seemed to respect her.

Smartgrrls manages its organization through two boards of directors—one composed of adults and one composed of girls. The girls' board conducts all their meetings online. They run their board the way they love the most—via chat and e-mail. "The girls just rock online," exclaimed Rachel. "They care about everything and have incredible discussions. I know that we are developing a real brand name here with Smartgrrls. I want our programs and ideas to reach as far as they can."

Rachel realizes the power the Internet has to offer her as a small organization. She is building a powerful community that initiates events not only in Austin, where Smartgrrls is based, but also throughout their virtual community. In April this year the organization initiated the "Virtual Take Your Daughter to Work Day" when girls from all over the U.S. shared their experience. Rachel knows she has touched a nerve, and this is beautifully reflected in how full of optimism and ideas she is.

"I am amazed sometimes to hear myself talk like a business executive. I have learned so much in the last two years. And I know now that we are going to make Smartgrrls a huge success," says Rachel with a big smile as we conclude our visit. The film crew is wrapping up, and 25 Smartgrrls are happily chatting as the summer camp activities come to a close. "They will all continue this on the Web," Rachel reassures us. "All of our girls stay in touch with each other and with us." She gets back on her bike and peddles away.

Esther Drill
Founder and executive director, gURL teen site
February 1999
www.gurl.com

When I first started researching girls' Web sites, I immediately took a liking to the www.gurl.com site. It was fresh and different and stood out as an example of what a good medium the Web can be for attracting girls to use technology,. so I emailed their Web master, Sonja, and got this reply:

hi —>

you know i think the people who can best represent &
talk about gURL are esther drill, heather mcdonald and
rebecca odes. The three of them started the project while
they were students of the Interactive Telecommunications
program at NYU. Esther and Rebecca have known each
other since they were maybe 3 or 4, and I think the spirit
of their friendship contributes much to the spirit of their
site (they are fantastically close, as close as they are
different, open, accepting and generally great to work
with). I do a lot of the production & programming on
the site —> the three of them, tho, are in charge of the
marketing, promotions, creative design, & know all the
details re: their relationship to delias... There are many,
many talented young women who contribute to the site
(including students at NYU, Columbia); people who I
think are both technologically & creatively brilliant,
socially and politically progressive. As for myself, I'm
hoping to see that some girls find it fuels their interest in
technology. But then esther, I think, may stress that it
serves to let girls experience a community of their own
design....

yours (best of luck with the book)
sja

So I decided to call up Esther Drill, the founder, and
talk to her about how she got to where she is today, a young
woman Internet trailblazer. Esther started as a New York University (NYU) masters student in the interactive telecommu-
nication program. She had personal stories she wanted to tell,
but she had no idea that anyone would want to hear them or
even notice her Web site that displayed them, yet — to her
surprise — when she first showed the Web site at an NYU

open house, she got a lot of press coverage.

It took six months to reach teenage girls to come to the site. Only after Elle, Harper's Bazaar, and Seventeen magazines wrote about the site in 1996/97 did it become well known. Esther had a best friend, Rebecca, with whom she had planned to do something in the media since high school. They had an idea to start a girls' magazine that would be different from anything they had seen before. When the Web magazine idea came about, they liked the fact that it was not going to be using print and they did not have to follow tradition or be under advertising pressure.

Esther admitted that she has always been good at math and said the NYU program was very supportive of non-computer experts, so she always got to ask technical questions of the people around her. The NYU masters program had plenty of women. Dr. Red Burns, the chairwoman, started the program in 1978 and still serves as a strong role model for women in the program. She was very supportive of what Esther and Rebecca did and made available the resources they needed to develop the Web site.

The Delia Company (the largest teen girls' catalog company in the U.S.) last December started talks with Esther and Rebecca, right after their graduation. They approached the two women because they were aware of the online community they had built in such a short time. Esther and Rebecca knew that with Delia's help, they would be able to reach a lot more people than on their own.

Now their Web site is in all Delia's catalogs, and there are plans to expand the site to a full e-commerce site. Delia's offices are in New York too, and they had given Esther and Rebecca and their staff offices in their building. The company plans to spin off the Internet group into a separate company. Esther and Rebecca do not deal much with the e-commerce site, but they do their promotions together with Delia. Membership is their main revenue stream but is not meant to bring in the lion's share of the income.

The women's best asset is in aggregating a community, and in that they do not have any real competitors. Teen girl magazines are coming online, but their content is very different from gurl and they lack the community experience. Girl Games is not really a competitor; it did not focus on a Web community and maybe that is why their Web site is not attracting as many girls as gurl. Aliza's Webgrrls is not really meant for networking. This is a very young industry, and there are not a lot of players yet. Being in New York has also been helpful because Esther and Rebecca get support and a sense of community.

Mentoring is one of the new goals for the gurl site; they are building a personal college database to help girls find matching people with similar goals. Also the database will help high-school girls with their choice of college.

Esther is happy to be spending energy on developing the site right now, but as far as the future is concerned, she is aware that all the senior managers at the Delia company are men. However, there are a lot of other opportunities, and there are now a lot of examples of successful women (such as the founders of iVillage and Oxygen) to follow. Esther knows that the Internet fits women's profile (communication ability), but it can be what anyone wants it to be. She is not that optimistic about women making it big on the Net, but she emphasizes that if women take advantage of the great opportunities the Net presents—anything can happen.

Conclusion

Women Weaving Webs: Taking Charge of Our Virtual Global Village

W hen I started writing this book, I dreamed that one day I would be reading this news:

> Like political candidates seeking out new voting niches, e-commerce companies are taking a hard look at the population of surfers and buyerson the web—and they are finding some significant shifts.
>
> For one thing, there are more women on the Web than ever. According to the latest figures from Jupiter Communications, women currently make up 49 percent of the 100 million internet users in the United States, and that figure will reach 50 percent by next year. Even more notably, Jupiter predicts that women will outspend men online within the next three years.
>
> —*InternetWeek Newsletter*
> Friday, November 5, 1999

Now that we have achieved parity in the U.S. as Internet users, we absolutely MUST spread the word to the rest of our global village. We must help women around the world join us in taking charge of this virtual environment. We must make them understand what we already know—that the internet has the capability of offering women — for the first time — a tool that perfectly mirrors their way of operating and thinking. The Internet's web-like structure is precisely the type women prefer when building their own social and organizational structures.

Women weave webs instinctively. They create structures that are inextricably integrated and connected. Those tend continually to be built up, stretched, altered, modified, and transformed. This incredible match between the Internet and women's way of thinking and organizing has not been discussed before.

Women view the Internet as one more technological obstacle they need to overcome. The essential message of this book is that they need to view the Net as a technology that—for the first time in history—can empower them to master technology in unprecedented ways! This book is a "call to arms" to all women to take charge of the Internet and make it work for them, for their local communities, and for their global community in ways that will proactively meet all their needs.

We have learned that:

1. We need to understand women's barriers to technology (specifically the Internet).
2. We need to learn how to overcome those barriers.
3. We need to recognize the natural link between women and the Internet.
4. Therefore, we need to take ownership of this technology!

The Internet is a different technology from any other computing technology to date. It is more suited to women's capabilities and is, consequently, an ideal tool for empowering women. With this book, I hope I have shown you that:

1. Women's traits and natural tendencies, match up remarkably with the Internet's traits.
2. The number of women on the Web is rapidly increasing worldwide and will soon surpass men's members in the U.S.
3. Companies online are now marketing specifically to women with very positive results.
4. The Internet has played a strong role in some recent women's success stories.
5. Women can harvest Internet technology for the good of their gender and communities.

I hope that the book has inspired you to take charge of this amazing technology See you in cyberspace!

Appendix A

Women Weaving Webs— A Personal Journey

When I first started thinking about writing this book to share the sense of empowerment I have derived from working on the Internet, I did so during a period of personal transformation in my life. I had been driven out of corporate America into the world of small business ownership and discovered many kindred souls in the process. This is the chronicle of the journey I took trying to make a reality of my idea of helping women embrace and master Internet technology, while transforming myself from a privileged professional to a struggling new business owner and crusader.

It all started in June of 1996 when my best friend, Julie, and I took off to go to North Carolina for a summer vacation. We had been planning this forever. Julie wanted to quit her government job and move to Asheville, the New Age Mecca. I wanted to have some time to work with Julie on a book idea I had about women and the Web. Both of us had had zero time to think about our futures, having been busy working on our doctoral dissertations while holding full-time jobs, yet we both felt the need to take time off to start planning the second chapter of our lives. North Carolina could prove to be a great place to rid ourselves of the corporate and government worlds' burdens. We could not wait to sit on top of the Smoky Mountains with our laptops nearby, weaving our thoughts away from the technocratic world of our everyday life into a whole new realm....

While in North Carolina we discovered the legend of the "dreamcatcher" through a Native American who worked at the retreat where we stayed. We both bought her handmade webs of dreams and hung them above our beds. The sight of the web swinging gently over my head at night formed a new idea in my mind... 'weaving webs'... 'we are weaving our webs'.... By the time we got back to the "real" world, a secret smile started appearing on my face every time I thought about the book I was planning. Somehow the dreamcatcher seemed to hold a magic spell over all my future plans. However, by wintertime every time I would look at the dreamcatcher hanging over my desk, I would sigh and think about the legend of the bad dreams getting caught in the web while the good ones slide into one's subconscious.... I could use some good dreams right now. I became so busy at work that the idea of ever writing a book about women and the Internet seemed more and more remote.

As I ventured deeper and deeper into the World Wide Web, my sanity was preserved through new connections I encountered on my exploratory journeys. And the joy I experienced taking those virtual journeys made me determined again to share what I found with other women. I started surfing the Net compulsively every day and tried to network with as many people as I could. As a result, I was introduced to the Department of Commerce's U.S. Aid program and was sent to Eastern Europe, where I delivered a series of seminars to the local people about the Internet. The level of interest was phenomenal! It was amazing to see how interconnected we have become and what tremendous impact the Internet holds for our global society.

In January of 1997, with the beginning of a new year, I resolved to sit down and start writing my book. By February I was out of a job due to corporate downsizing. I decided I would join the vast number of new women business owners who were looking at the Internet as their new frontier for developing their business. As I struggled to become an independent Internet consultant, I started getting approached by other women business owners who wanted me to tell them how they could use the Internet to transform their companies. One of the women suggested that I talk to our community center about holding some women's workshops in conjunction with writing my book in order to get some feedback from "real" women on their experience with the Net. And that's how the Women.Weaving.Webs project got started!

The Houston Business Women's Council decided to help promote the project with all their members and supporters. Many women rallied to help put the workshops together. It was as if Internet fever was everywhere! In May of 1997 I got back from a visit to Japan. The Internet, I discovered, was BIG news there, in spite of the fact that it was very costly to connect to. While in Japan I visited an Internet café that was full of young girls busy surfing on the Net and writing e-mail, yet when I discussed the Internet with Maria, my Japanese interpreter, the true picture emerged — women are the very last to get on the Internet in Japan. Since they are also scarce in any position of power in the workforce, they rarely get the privilege of access to the Net.

As summer approached, I became involved with The Association of Women in Computing, who agreed to sponsor one of my workshops. Their support became invaluable in propelling me to grow my Internet business. During the summer I also had an opportunity to visit Julie in North Carolina. She has quit her government job and started a Web design business in Asheville. I became one of her first clients.

By the end of 1997 we had an opportunity to run our first girls' workshop. More than 75 junior high-school girls showed up! During the same time we also collaborated with our local book fair in putting together the first Internet Day for the community. It was a great success! Hundreds of people of all ages came to our demo area. We set up work stations and manned them with volunteers to discuss Internet sites for women, kids, teens, community volunteers, senior citizens, and more. We had a series of seminars going on concurrently and discussed issues such as how to create your Web presence and how to navigate the Net safely.

With New Year's Day of 1998 came the resolution to continue my crusade to get as many women using the Internet as I could influence. During the year I gave lectures in many small and large meetings and continued to talk informally to all my fellow women business owners. I also sat down and wrote a good portion of the book. As I continued with my research towards the end of 1998, I was getting very encouraged seeing the numbers of women online growing rapidly. I knew then that the tide had turned. We were taking charge of our virtual global village. And my dreams were finally getting caught in my dreamcatcher and becoming a reality....

Appendix B

Recommended Reading—
Women and Technology

Atkinson, Steven D., and Judith Hudson, eds. *Women Online: Research In Women's Studies Using Online Databases.* New York: Haworth Press, 1990.

Balsamo, Anne. *Technologies of the Gendered Body: Reading Cyborg Women.* Durham, NC: Duke University Press, 1995.

"Beyond Barbie: Games by Women." *The New York Times,* November 11, 1996.

Bitter, Gary G. "Technology and Minorities: A Local Program Aimed at Increasing Technological Capabilities of Hispanic Women." *Computers in the Schools 9,* no.1 (1992).

Calabrese, Andrew. "Home-based Telework and the Politics of Private Woman and Public Man: A Critical Appraisal." *Women and Technology,* Urs E. Gattiker, ed. New York: Walter de Gruyter, 1994.

Camp, Tracy. "The incredible shrinking pipeline" *Communications of the ACM 40,* no. 10 (1997).

Cardman, Elizabeth. "The Gender Gap in Computer Use:

Implications for Bibliographic Instruction." *Research Strategies* 8, no.3 (1990).

Cherny, Lynn, and Elizabeth Reba Weise, eds. *Wired Women: Gender and New Realities in Cyberspace* Seattle: Seal Press, 1996.

Clarke, Valerie, I*n Search of Gender Free Paradigms for Computer Science Education*, C. Dianne Martin and Eric Murchie-Beyma, eds. Eugene, Oregon: International Society for Technology in Education, 1992.

Clerc, Susan. "Estrogen Brigades and 'Big Tits' Threads: Media Fandom Online and Off" in Lynn Cherny and Elizabeth Weise, eds. *wired_women,* Washington: Seal Press, 1996.

Cockburn, Cynthia. "Domestic technologies: Cinderella and the engineers." *Women's Studies International Forum 20*, no. 3 (1997).

Cottrell, Janet. "I'm a stranger here myself: A consideration of women in computing." *iLearning from the Past, Stepping into the Future, the Proceedings of the 1992 ACM SIGUCCS User Services Conference, November 8-11,1992, Cleveland, OH,* New York: The Association for Computing Machinery, 1992.

Cultures of Computing, The, Star, Susan Leigh, ed. Oxford: Basil Blackwell, 1995.

Dibble, Julian. "A Rape in Cyberspace: A Tale of Crime and Punishment On-Line." *The Village Voice,* December 21, 1993.

Dietrich, Dawn., "(Re)-Fashioning the Techno-Erotic Woman: Gender and Textuality in the Cybercultural Matrix" in Steven

Jones, ed. *Virtual Culture*. London: Sage, 1997.

Doing It the Hard Way: Investigations of Gender and Technology, Sally Hacker, D. Smith, and S. Turner, eds. London: Unwin Hyman, 1990.

Feminist Collections: A Quarterly of Women's Studies Resources 17, No.2 (winter 1996); special issue: "Information Technology and Women's Studies: Reports from the Field," eds. Phyllis Holman Weisbard and Linda Shult.

Freeman, Elisabeth, and Susanne Hupfer. "TAP: Tapping Internet Resources for Women in Computing." *Communications of the ACM 38*, No.1 (January 1995).

Frissen, Valerie. "Trapped in electronic cages? Gender and new information technologies in the public and private domain: an overview of research," *Media, Culture and Society 14*, No. 1 (1992).

Gailey, Christine Ward. "Mediated Messages: Gender, Class, and Cosmos in Home Video Games." *Journal of Popular Culture 27* (summer 1993).

Gray, Chris Hables, et al. "Cyborgology: Constructing the knowledge of cybernetic organisms" in *The Cyborg Handbook*, C. H. Gray, ed. London: Routledge, 1995.

Hapnes, Tove, and Knut H. Sorensen. "Competition and Collaboration in Male Shaping of Computing: A Study of a Norwegian Hacker Culture." *The Gender-Technology Relation: Contemporary Theory and Research*, Keith Grint and Rosalind Gill, eds. Briston, Pennsylvania: Taylor & Francis, 1995.

Haraway, Donna. Simians. *Cyborgs and Women: The Reinvention of Nature.* London: Free Association Books, 1991.

Hawkins , Jan. "Computers and Girls: Rethinking the Issues," *Sex Roles,* 13 (1985).

Herring, Susan, Deborah A. Johnson, and Tamra DiBenedetto. "This discussion is going too far!: Male resistance to female participation on the Internet" in *Gender Articulated. Language and the Socially Constructed Self,* Kira Hall and Mary Bucholtz, eds. London: Routledge, 1995.

Hossfeld, Karen J. "'Their Logic Against Them': Contradictions in Sex, Race, and Class in Silicon Valley." *Women Workers and Global Restructuring.* Kathryn Ward, ed. Ithaca, New York: ILR Press, 1990.

Huff, Charles W., and Joel Cooper. "Sex bias in educational software: The effect of designers' stereotypes on the software they design," *Journal of Applied Social Psychology 17,* No. 6 (1987).

Huff, Charles W., John H. Fleming, and Joel Cooper "Gender differences in human-computer interaction," in *In Search of Gender Free Paradigms for Computer Science Education,* C. Dianne Martin and Eric Murchie-Beyma, eds. Eugene, Oregon: International Society for Technology in Education, 1992.

Jacobson, Frances F. "Gender Differences in Attitudes toward Using Computers in Libraries: An Exploratory Study." *Library and Information Science Research 13,* No. 3 (July-September 1991).

Jantzen, Gitte, and Jans F. Jensen. "Powerplay—Power, violence and gender in video games," *AI and Society 7*, (1993).

"Japan's Newest Heartthrobs Are Sexy, Talented, and Virtual." *The New York Times*, November 25, 1996.

Kaplan, Nancy, and Eva Farrell.. "Weavers of Webs: A Portrait of Young Women on the Net." *The Arachnet Electronic Journal on Virtual Culture 2.3*, (1994).

Kendall, Lori., "MUDder? I Hardly Know 'Er! Adventures of a Feminist MUDder" in Lynn Cherny and Elizabeth Weise, eds. *wired_women*, Washington: Seal Press, 1996.

Kiesler , Sara, and Lee Sproull. "Pool Halls, Chips, and War Games: Women in the Culture of Computing," *Psychology of Women Quarterly 9*, (1984).

Kiesler, Sara, Lee Sproull, and Jacquelynne Eccles. "Pool halls, chips, and war games: Women in the culture of computing," *Psychology of Women Quarterly 9*, (1985).

Kramarae, Cheris. "A backstage critique of virtual reality" in *Cybersociety: Computer-mediated Communication and Community*, Steven G. Jones, ed. London: Sage, 1995.

Kramarae, Cheris. "Gotta Go Myrtle, Technology's at the Door." *Technology and Women's Voices: Keeping in Touch*. Cheris Kramarae, ed. New York: Routledge, 1988.

Light, Jennifer. "The Digital Landscape: A New Place for Women," *Gender, Place, and Culture 2*, No. 2 (September

1995).

Makrakis, Vasilios. "Gender and Computing in Schools in Japan: The 'We Can, I Can't' Paradox." *Computers and Education 20,* (March 1993).

Markussen, Randi. "Constructing Easiness — Historical Perspectives on Work, Computerization, and Women." *The Cultures of Computing.* Susan Leigh Star, ed. Oxford: Blackwell Publishers, 1995.

Martin, Michle. *Gender, Technology and Culture in the Formation of Telephone Systems.* Montreal: McGill-Queen's University Press, 1991.

Miller, Laura. "Women and Children First: Gender and the Settling of the Electronic Frontier." *Resisting the Virtual Life: The Culture and Politics of Information.* James Brook and Iain Boal, eds. San Francisco: City Lights Books, 1995.

Mitter , Swasti, and Sheila Robotham, eds. *Women Encounter Technology*, New York: Routledge, 1995.

Pearl, A., et al. "Becoming a computer scientist: A report by the ACM Committee on the status of women in computing science," *Communications of the ACM 33,* No. 11 (1990).

Penley, Constance. "Brownian Motion: Women, Tactics, and Technology." *Technoculture,* Constance Penley and Andrew Ross, eds. Minneapolis: University of Minnesota Press, 1991.

Perenson, Melissa J., et al. "What Do Women Want?: Software for Women and Girls." *PC Magazine 13,* No. 19 (November 8, 1994).

Provenzo Jr., Eugene F. "The portrayal of women," in *Video*

Kids: Making Sense of Nintendo, Cambridge, Massachusetts: Harvard University Press, 1991.

Ross, Andrew. "Cyberpunk in Boystown" in *Strange Weather: Culture, Science, and Technology in the Age of Limits,* New York: Verso, 1991.

Schuler, Douglas. "What is a community network?" in *New Community Networks: Wired for Change,* New York: ACM Press, 1996.

Spender, Dale, *Nattering on the Net: Women, Power and Multimedia,* North Melbourne, Australia: Spinifex, 1995.

Springer, Claudia. "Sex, Memories, and Angry Women." *Flame Wars: The Discourse of Cyberculture,* Mark Dery, ed. Durham: Duke University Press, 1994.

Stabile, Carol, *Feminism and the Technological Fix,* Manchester, England: Manchester University Press, 1994.

Star, Susan Leigh. "From Hestia to Home Page: Feminism and the Concept of Home in Cyberspace" in Nina Lykke and Rosi Braidotti, eds. Between *Monsters, Goddesses and Cyborgs,* London: ZED Books, 1996.

Strok, Dale. "Women in AI," *IEEE Expert 7,* No. 4 (1992): 7-10.

Turkle, Sherry. "Constructions and reconstructions of self in virtual reality: Playing in the MUDs" in *Mind, Culture and Activity 1,* (1994).

Turkle, Sherry. "Hackers; loving the machine for itself" in *The Second Self,* New York: Simon and Schuster, 1984.

Turkle, Sherry, *Life on the Screen: Identity in the Age of the Internet*, New York: Simon and Schuster, 1995.

"Understanding community in the information age," in *Cybersociety: Computer-mediated Communication and Community*, Steven G. Jones, ed. London: Sage, 1995.

Wagner, Ina. "Women's Voice: The Case of Nursing Information Systems," *AI and Society 7*, No. 4 (August 1995).

Wagner, Ina. "Hard Times: The Politics of Women's Work in Computerized Environments." *Women, Work and Computerization: Breaking Old Boundaries, Building New Forms.* Alison Adam, ed. Amsterdam: Elsevier, 1994.

Wajcman, Judy, *Feminism Confronts Technology*, University Park: Pennsylvania State University Press, 1991.

War of Desire and Technology at the Close of the Mechanical Age, The, Cambridge, Massachusetts: MIT Press, 1995.

Webster, Juliet. "What Do We Know about Gender and Information Technology at Work? A Discussion of Selected Feminist Research." *European Journal of Women's Studies 2*, No. 3 (August 1995).

Zimmerman, Jan. "Technology and the Future of Women: Haven't We Met Somewhere Before?" *Women's Studies International Quarterly 4*, (1981).

Appendix C

My Top 100 Web Sites
About Women and for Women

*N*ewsweek reported that as of August 1999 there are approximately 800 million pages on the Web. The following 100 Web sites are a few that I came upon during my personal journey through the virtual world. They are listed here in no particular order, in a Web-like fashion, just the way I have discovered them.

Since using search engines with keywords like "women" or "girls" to find sites like these will invariably lead you to thousands of pornographic sites, I wanted to make your journey a little easier and less overwhelming. I hope you find this list both helpful and useful. Each site address is accompanied by a description taken directly from the site itself whenever possible.

Feel free to e-mail your list of favorite sites to me at *info@weavingwebs.com* so that they may be included in this book's upcoming new edition.

1. *women.weaving.webs.com*
    A site dedicated to the Women.Weaving.Webs project run by the author to help women reach a critical mass on the Web.

2. *www.oxygen.com*

   A site set out to create a new kind of relationship between women and the media that serve us—one based on honesty, humor, and heart. The creators of the site think of this as a shared adventure, a work in progress inspired and powered by you and them together.

3. *www.womenconnect.com*

   WomenConnect.com is a community of professional women and women business owners that provides relevant information, networking opportunities, interactive discussions among peers and with guest experts, and value-added products and services for women's personal and business needs.

4. *www.women.com*

   Women.com is the leading network for wired women, attracting more than 4 million visitors each month. Founded in 1992 when "women online" was something of a novelty, Women.com Networks provides a unique blend of content, community, commerce, and services that serves the diverse needs of today's online woman.

5. *www.womenswire.com*

   A site affiliated with women.com that includes many chat areas and message boards on various topics.

6. *www.witi.com*

   Women in Technology International's goal is to

empower its constituents by providing access to people and content which are relevant to the issues faced by women in technology.

7. *www.amazoncity.com*
    A full-featured online community for women on the Web with original content, discussion forums, chat rooms, unique community services, and a distinct flair.

8. *www.electra.com*
    An affiliate site of Oxygen.com, this site offers content and community on topics ranging from money issues to dating.

9. *www.hersalon.com*
    The "cyber theme park" for women.

10. *www.ivillage.com*
    The most visited women's network/portal on the Web.

11. *www.lasmujeres.com*
    The site features profiles of prominent Latina women.

12. *www.oprah.com*
    A Web site covering the Oprah show and following the show's main themes.

13. *www.kotex.com*
    A site designed for young women to help them feel more comfortable with their bodies.

14. *www.womenfolk.com*
A site where women get together to share their creativity and inspiration.

15. *www.hbwm.com*
Home-Based Working MomsTM is a national association for parents who work at home. HBWM is an advocate of home employment and home business to allow parents to spend more time with their children.

16. *www.asiangurls.com*
This is a Web site devoted to high quality content for intelligent people. It provides resources, forums, and discussions about things that interest Asian and Asian-American women.

17. *www.wwwomen.com*
The most inclusive, up-to-date search site for women's topics. It is dedicated to finding all sites on the Web relevant to women—from sites about child rearing and pregnancy to sites about civil liberties, careers, and religion.

18. *www.femina.com*
This site provides women with a comprehensive, searchable directory of links to female-friendly sites and information on the World Wide Web.

19. *www.phenomenalwomen.com*
This site is a directory of sites which have earned the seal and membership given to Women and Young Women on the Internet with outstanding

pages; they also designate "pages of Excellence" and "Honor" categories.

20. *www.seniorwomen.com*
    The site is for women over 50. "Senior," in this case, means women who have graduated from one stage of life to another. The site was fashioned to focus on women's political, health, fitness, and monetary issues as well as to reflect on lifestyles.

21. *www.chickclick.com*
    A collection of Web sites for women and girls who "don't fake it."

22. *www.estronet.com*
    Part of the chickclick.com sites meant for older "chicks."

23. *www.girlgeeks.com*
    This site promotes women in computing—past, present, and future—through interactive Web sites, TV, radio, books, and educational and mentoring services and products.

24. *www.top25.org*
    The Top25 Women on the Web awards are unique in recognizing the achievements of 25 women who have most inspired people worldwide with their efforts to advance technology, contribute to the community, and set an example as successful businesswomen in the Internet and new media industries.

25. *www.webmistressatwork.com*
This site supports a community atmosphere in which women in business can ask questions, find answers, and get help and support on issues confronting their online business endeavors.

26. *www.wowwomen.com*
This site was created as a global community where women of all races, religions, cultures, and orientations can unite in a cyber-sisterhood. Women's voices, feelings, and wisdom are valued and shared here.

27. *www.cybergrrl.com*
This site is dedicated to informing, inspiring, and celebrating women through shared content with its community of users.

28. *women.msn.com*
A comprehensive women's portal that includes many content areas, shopping, and chat rooms.

29. *www.planetgrrl.com*
This site is a resource by women and girls from the U.K. in or interested in new media and technology "for chicks everywhere."

30. *www.russianwebgirls.com*
A virtual club that redefines the term "Russian women" and increases their presence on the Internet (in English and Russian).

31. *www.webgrrls.com*

    Webgrrls International provides a forum for women in or interested in new media and technology to network, exchange job and business leads, form strategic alliances, mentor and teach, and intern and learn the skills to help women succeed in an increasingly technical workplace and world.

32. *www.herdomain.org*

    A support and networking group for women in the Austin, Texas, area, interested in the World Wide Web.

33. *www.awc-hq.org*

    The national site of the Association for Women in Computing.

34. *www.globalfundforwomen.org*

    The Global Fund for Women makes grants to seed, support, and strengthen women's rights groups around the world.

35. *www.iwpr.org*

    The Institute for Women's Policy Research (IWPR) is an independent, nonprofit, scientific research organization, established in 1987 to rectify the limited availability of policy-relevant research on women's lives and to inform and stimulate debate on issues of critical importance for women.

36. *sisters-in-sisters.org*
Sisters International®, Inc. is an organization for women who believe they can change the world for the better. It's about developing healthy families and communities by building on the innate strengths that women have and encouraging their practice in everyday life.

37. *www.wlo.org*
Women Leaders Online is the first and largest women's activist group on the internet—empowering women in politics, media, society, the economy, and cyberspace.

38. *www.wilpf.org*
Women's International League for Peace and Freedom works to achieve through peaceful means world disarmament, a sustainable environment, and an end to all forms of violence and to establish those economic, political, social, and psychological conditions which can assure peace, freedom, women's rights, racial and economic justice, and justice for all.

39. *www.about-face.org*
About-Face is a media literacy organization focused on the impact mass media has on the physical, mental, and emotional well-being of women and girls. Through practical and activist methods, they challenge our culture's overemphasis on physical appearance. By encouraging critical thinking about the media and personal empowerment, About-Face works to engender positive

body-esteem in girls and women of all ages, sizes, races, and backgrounds.

40. *www.awis.org*
    A site for The Association for Women in Science that is dedicated to the achievement of equity and full participation of women in all areas of science and technology.

41. *www.nawbo.org*
    A site for the National Association for Women Business Owners.

42. *www.now.org*
    A site for the National Organization of Women.

43. *www.rockrgrl.com*
    Online companion to ROCKRGRL Magazine. Readers are treated to intelligent interviews with exceptional women of note from Ani to Yoko as well as poignant essays. Topics include "How To Start a Label," "Booking Your Own Tour," legal issues, gear, studio tips, and more.

44. *www.gogirlsmusic.com*
    A site dedicated to the world of indie music. Here you will find tons of info on women-fronted and all-girl bands. It ranges from rock to pop, ska to metal, and everything in between.

45. *www.girlpress.com*
    Girl Press is dedicated to creating books for girls that will make them strong, self-reliant, and ready for life's adventure.

46. *www.the-womens-press.com*
The site of a U.K.-based publishing house specializing in "books of integrity by women writers."

47. *www.smartgrrl.com*
This nonprofit organization's objective is to collaborate with parents, schools, higher education, industry, and community groups to provide programs, strategies, and resources to increase the interest of young women in math, science, engineering, and technology fields.

48. *www.ms.foundation.org*
The site of the Ms. Foundation, which supports the efforts of women and girls to govern their own lives and influence the world around them. The foundation funds and assists women's self-help organizing efforts and pursues changes in public consciousness, law, philanthropy, and social policy.

49. *www.womenshealth.org*
A Forum for Women's Health addresses a variety of issues concerning women's health from sports and fitness to beauty, healthcare, diet, and nutrition, among others.

50. *www.womens-health.com*
The Women's Health Interactive is an interactive learning environment that facilitates the exchange of information among all participants, promotes learning, and motivates individual proactive response.

51. *www.womenshealthnet.com*
Through their e-zine channels, this site will cover health and wellness from A to Z so you can find everything you need. What makes it unique is that it will also provide you with a direct connection to the most forward-thinking medical practices across the nation.

52. *www.thewhitehouseproject.org*
The White House Project is working to change the U.S. political climate so women from all walks of life can launch successful campaigns for the U.S. presidency and other key positions.

53. *www.thecybermom.com*
A home on the Net for moms with modems. An active community dealing with motherhood-related issues.

54. *www.momsonline.com*
Moms Online is a virtual community of mothers working collaboratively to create a friendly site for moms in cyberspace. By "mom" they include anyone engaged in nurturing the next generation—from stay-at-home moms to working moms, married moms to single moms, teen moms to grandmoms to dads.

55. *www.worldwoman.net*
The first virtual women's newspaper in the world, whose goal is to know what's happening to the 51% of the population other papers tend to forget. They find new stories, develop new perspec-

tives, make new links, tell new jokes, and above all find solutions to the problems the male managers of this millenium have found intractable.

56. *www.latina.com*
An online version of the magazine for Latin women.

57. *www.voiceofwomen.com*
This site offers articles on a wide variety of topics, a calendar of events, bridges to other destinations on the Web, a directory of woman-friendly businesses, and a marketplace as tools to empower women users.

58. *www.herspace.com*
The Herspace Network is a unique network of diverse Web sites for women such as those for women writers and women travelers.

59. *www.electrasports.com*
The most comprehensive online collection of women's sports apparel and a place to share your sports-related experiences.

60. *www.gURL.com*
A rich online environment for girls and young women to chat, read, and shop (at delia.com, its affiliate e-commerce site).

61. *www.bguide.com*
The Beatrice Web Guide, another woman.com affiliate portal that also links in to many women's

magazines like Good Housekeeping.

62. *women.astrology.net*
A site specifically about female issues, energy, roles, and astrology. It was created in order to help women understand themselves better through the mythology of astrology.

63. *www.icrw.org*
The International Center for Research on Women is a private, nonprofit organization dedicated to promoting social and economic development with women's full participation.

64. *www.shu.ac.uk/witec*
A European site for the Association for Women in Technology, Engineering, and Science.

65. *www.iwt.org*
The Institute for Women and Technology exists to increase the impact of women on technology and in education, design, development, deployment, and policy; to increase the positive impact of technology on the lives of all women; and to help communities, industry, education, and governments accelerate and benefit from these increases.

66. *www.wiredwoman.com*
The Wired Woman Society is a nonprofit group where women can learn and share ideas about new media technology in a comfortable and dynamic online space.

67. *quest.arc.nasa.gov/women*
A National Aeronautics and Space Administration tribute to the women astronauts including full biographies and pictures.

68. *www.womenjapan.com*
A portal for Japanese women full of content and shopping.

69. *www.pleiades-net.com*
Pleiades Networks is a place for women to convene and share ideas in a comfortable and engaging environment. Their goal is to create a community of women who share their knowledge and experience to help each other learn and grow as individuals.

70. *www.anincomeofherown.com*
The Independent Means Web site is the place for women under 20 (and their over-20 mentors) to find an income of their own. It is also a provider of products and services for girls' financial independence. They are the first stop for news on starting a business; making, saving, and growing money; and networking with mentors.

71. *www.girlscouts.org/girls*
This is the "just for girls" portion of the Girl Scouts Web site, where girls can do things such as chat and ask questions of experts.

72. *www.nrrdgrrl.com*
Nerd Girl is for all the girls who might look like

the girl next door but are fed up with women's magazines trying to tell them they need fixing and will never be "just right."

73. *www.terrifichick.com*
The site strives to be truly alternative: helping young girls be and do whatever they think is cool. It tries to give young girls the straight facts on what they want to know, without being dull. They want to help them look at all the images that surround them, from magazines, TV shows, movies—and even the Internet— and help them see through the hype.

74. *www.wnba.com*
This is the official WNBA site that is meant for all women basketball lovers and men loving women's basketball.

75. *www.lifetimetv.com*
This site covers the shows on the women's television channel but also has exclusive online interactive content and online community.

76. *www.africaonline.com/AfricaOnline/ coverwomen.html*
This portion of Africa Online is dedicated to African women and covers more than seven African nations.

77. *www.aviva.org*
AVIVA is a '"Webzine," being run by an international group of women based in London. They

are providing a free listings service for women everywhere, funded by advertising and sponsorship.

78. *www.femiweb.com*
   This is a French Web site for mothers, dealing with family issues in general and parental issues in particular.

79. *www.neww.org*
   The Network of East-West Women links women across national and regional boundaries to share resources, knowledge, and skills. Its mission is to empower women and girls throughout the East (Central and Eastern Europe and the Russian federation) and the West by dialogue, networking, campaigns, and educational and informational exchanges. NEWW supports action and joint projects inspired by feminist principles.

80. *www.twib.net*
   Texas Women in Business is informative, in-depth, entertaining, racy, and visual. It is the "It's about time!" publication for the Texas business-woman that tells her story and the bumpy road she traveled to achieve professional success.

81. *www.sem.or.cr*
   The Servicio Especial de la Mujer (SEM) is an international news agency staffed by women journalists from all over Latin America who write news articles and features with a gender perspective.

82. *www.womenconnect.org.uk*
This is the first U.K.-based women's Internet networking project. Women Connect aims to build organizational capacity for the future by strengthening all women's organizations and what they do in their communities.

83. *community.web.net/womensweb*
WomensWeb works to build the capacity of the Canadian women's movement to use the Internet to collaborate and further its aims. They are a national outreach and support program committed to developing a community of Canadian women's organizations online.

84. *www.women.ca*
This Web site serves as a resource center and meeting place for Canadian women. The Information Resource Center contains hundreds of links to sites relevant to women, with a special focus on Canadian content.

85. *www.newmoon.org*
New Moon is where girls tell the world who they are, without adults or advertisers as interpreters. It is a place where girls and adults work hand-in-hand, as peers, to create a publication that gives girls a chance to explore themselves, their dreams, and their ideas.

86. *www.nwhp.org*
The National Women's History Project is a non-profit corporation that established National

Women's History Month in 1980; maintains the clearinghouse for U.S. women's history information; issues a seasonal catalog of women's history posters, books, and materials; produces videos, posters, guides, and supplies for school and workplace; conducts in-service training for school teachers; and coordinates the Women's History Network.

87. *www.womenwriters.net*
An E-Zine dedicated to women writers from the 19th century till today with more than 300 links to women-created content.

88. *www.emilyslist.org*
An acronym for "Early Money Is Like Yeast" (it makes the dough rise), EMILY's List identifies viable pro-choice Democratic women candidates for key federal and statewide offices and supports them through financial contribution and seeking women voters.

89. *www.greatwomen.org*
The National Women's Hall of Fame located in New York state uses this site to give you a virtual tour of their museum.

90. *www.digital-women.com*
Digital-Women was created for women in business, businesswomen, and all women around the globe looking for a place to gather resources, free business tips, free sales tips, free marketing tips, and home business ideas and a place to network

with other businesswomen and women-owned businesses.

91. *www.advancingwomen.com*
    An international business and career online community with news and networking and strategy content for women.

92. *www.iwmf.org*
    The International Women's Media Foundation (IWMF) was launched in 1990 with a mission to strengthen the role of women in the news media worldwide, based on the belief that no press is truly free unless women share an equal voice.

93. *www.sba.gov/womeninbusiness*
    With a network of women's business owner representatives in every district office, more than 100 mentoring roundtables, and women-owned venture capital companies, nearly 70 women's business centers in 40 states, and the Online Women's Business Center on the Internet, OWBO is helping women start and build successful businesses.

94. *www.usia.gov/vitalvoices*
    Vital Voices is an ongoing global initiative which implements U.S. Secretary of State Madeleine Albright's commitment to promote the advancement of women as a U.S. foreign policy objective. It is creating unprecedented partnerships among governments, nongovernmental organizations, and the private sector to support the full

participation of women in the economic, social, and political progress of their countries.

95. *www.careerbabe.com*
This site is a personal career advisor for the online job search arena. Here you'll find tips on how to maximize your job search with the best online activities, resume writing tutorials, interview and salary negotiating tips, and career transition information.

96. *www.feminist.com*
If you're a feminist lost in cyberspace; how do you cut through the endless wilds of data and find women-friendly space? This site proclaims to be "the guiding light for progressive women on the Web."

97. *www.wwn.on.ca*
An online interactive community for women, one where they can educate each other by providing real-life content and empowering women with the knowledge required to make wise choices. Their goal is to become a community leader by contributing to women's awareness.

98. *gallery.uunet.be/internetpress/women.htm*
A large listing of many women's magazine and newsletters online as well as Internet radio and television offering female content.

99. *www.womensoccer.com*
The site for all content relating to women's soccer all over the world.

100. *www.systers.org*

An informal organization for technical women in computing that began in 1987 as a small mailing list for women in "systems", thus the name systers. There are now over 2500 systers in 38 countries. If you are a woman in the technical end of computing, you are welcome to join.